# EXTRAORDINARY PLACES
*… Close to London*

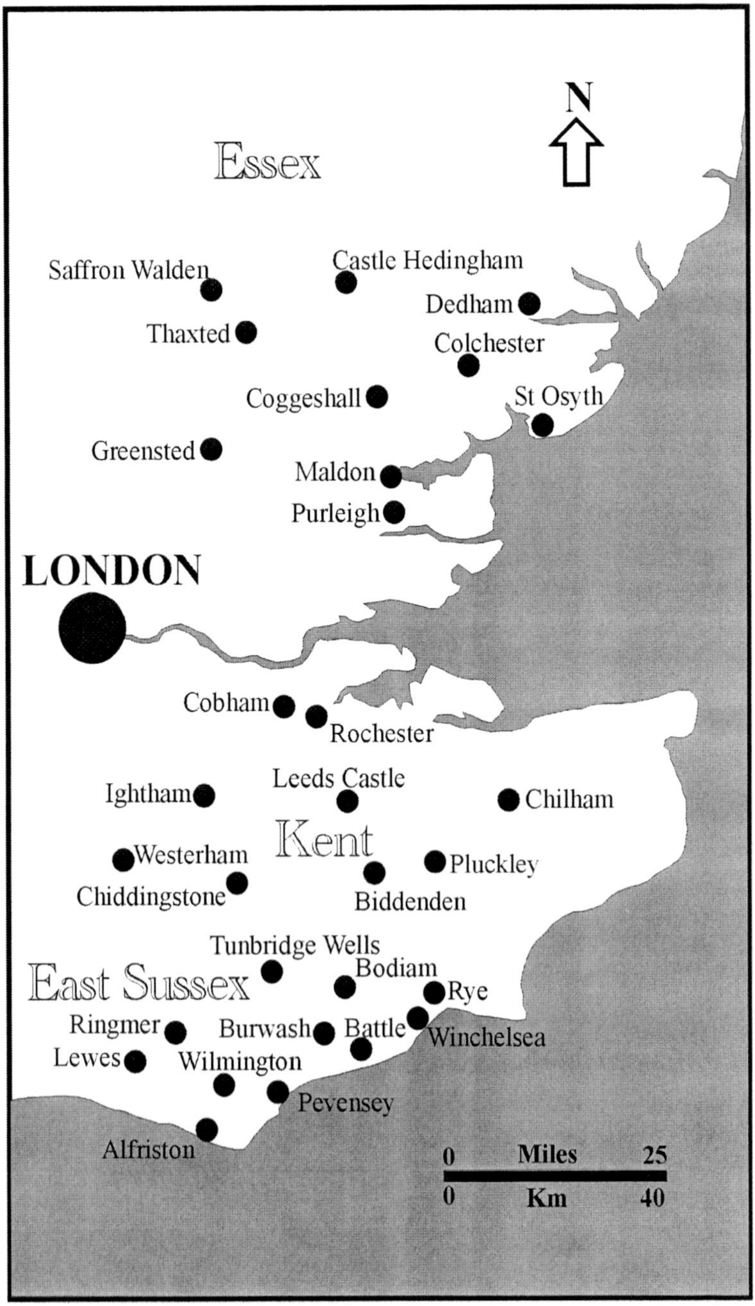

N
Essex
Saffron Walden
Castle Hedingham
Dedham
Thaxted
Colchester
Coggeshall
St Osyth
Greensted
Maldon
Purleigh
LONDON
Cobham
Rochester
Leeds Castle
Ightham
Chilham
Kent
Westerham
Pluckley
Chiddingstone
Biddenden
Tunbridge Wells
East Sussex
Bodiam
Rye
Ringmer
Burwash
Battle
Winchelsea
Lewes
Wilmington
Pevensey
Alfriston
0 Miles 25
0 Km 40

# EXTRAORDINARY PLACES
*... Close to London*

ELIZABETH  WALLACE

A *Daytrips* TRAVEL DISCOVERY BOOK

HASTINGS HOUSE
*Book Publishers*
Fern Park, Florida

While every effort has been made to insure accuracy, neither the author nor the publisher assume legal responsibility for any consequences arising from the use of this book or the information it contains.

Copyright © 2004 by Elizabeth Victoria Wallace.

All rights reserved. No part of this publication may be reproduced, stored in a retrieval system, or transmitted, in any form or by any means, electronic, mechanical, photocopying, recording, or otherwise, without the prior permission of the copyright owner or the publishers.

Inside photos by the author.
Cover photo by Earl Steinbicker.
Edited by Earl Steinbicker.
Peter Leers, Publisher.

www.DaytripsBooks.com
E-mail: Hastings_Daytrips@earthlink.net
ISBN: 0-8038-2031-3

*Printed in the United States of America*
10 9 8 7 6 5 4 3 2 1

# *Contents*

**Introduction**      1

## Essex

| | |
|---|---:|
| Purleigh | 5 |
| Maldon | 12 |
| Dedham | 20 |
| St. Osyth | 26 |
| Coggeshall | 33 |
| Colchester | 41 |
| Greensted | 49 |
| Castle Hedingham | 56 |
| Saffron Walden | 64 |
| Thaxted | 71 |

## Kent

| | |
|---|---:|
| Cobham | 78 |
| Royal Tunbridge Wells | 86 |
| Westerham | 93 |
| Ightham | 102 |
| Rochester | 109 |

| | |
|---|---|
| Chiddingstone | 119 |
| Pluckley | 128 |
| Chilham | 135 |
| Biddenden | 144 |
| Leeds Castle | 151 |

## East Sussex

| | |
|---|---|
| Burwash | 159 |
| Rye | 167 |
| Winchelsea | 175 |
| Bodiam | 184 |
| Battle | 192 |
| Lewes | 199 |
| Alfriston | 208 |
| Wilmington | 217 |
| Pevensey | 226 |
| Ringmer | 236 |

**Index** 244

# *Introduction*

This book is a personal and unique view into the life and history of the counties around London known as the Home Counties. Most of the villages and towns I know personally, some I had the pleasure of discovering for the first time while writing the book. This is a book for the more adventurous, sophisticated traveler who wants to explore little-known villages and towns in the English countryside, all within easy reach of London.

The counties covered are Essex, Kent, and East Sussex. Although most destinations can be reached by a short drive from London, you may consider using one of the towns as a base. Or perhaps choose to stay in a seaside B&B in East Sussex, where it is possible to take a brisk walk by the sea first thing in the morning before setting out.

The villages and towns I have chosen for this book tell stories of lesser-known and yet interesting and exciting places to visit. They are steeped in mystery and legend, including stories of kings and queens, Norsemen and witches.

You'll find a wonderful story of Saint Osyth, who lost her head to Danish pirates because she would not accept their pagan god. There is a story of Lawrence Washington, whose sons, disillusioned with their father's treatment by opponents of the king, emigrated to the New World and whose descendant became the first president of the United States.

John Constable wrote, "I love every stile and stump and lane…" Dedham, the village that Constable described and often painted, has changed little over the years. Dedham Church and the river Stour provide a wonderful setting for walks ranging from three to five miles. Dedham is also the home of the Sherman family, whose descendants became prominent in American history.

Kent is known as the Garden of England, but it was also called "the most civilized part of Britain" by Julius Caesar in 55 B.C. Some of the castles in Kent are said to be the most beautiful in the world and offer a sharp contrast to the hop fields, fruit farms, villages and oast houses of modern Kent.

On the 14th of October in 1066, William the Conqueror landed at Pevensey in East Sussex and marched inland six miles to the famous battle with King Harold. The town still bears the name of Battle. It's a busy town with antique and book shops, pubs and inns, all of which blend nicely with the Abbey Ruins and other ancient buildings. An impressive gate house leading to the abbey grounds lies at the head of Battle High Street.

In some chapters, you will see mention of *The Domesday Book*. This book was begun in 1086, 20 years after William the Conqueror landed in England. Its purpose was to provide a detailed account of the land, its citizens, and livestock against which a tax could be levied. So feared were the inhabitants of Britain by the development of such an inventory that they named the book *The Domesday Book*, from God's Final Day of Judgment.

I hope you will enjoy this book. I have tried to offer a rare insight to the history of each village and town to provide not only a travel guide but also a companion book that will enhance your visit to my native country, England.

# *Dedication*

I dedicate this book to my dear husband Donald, my three sons and their wonderful wives and children.

# *Essex*

## Purleigh

Purleigh is a small hamlet in the heart of Essex, located between the rivers Crouch and Blackwater, which has strong ties to the United States. The Reverend Lawrence Washington, who was forced to resign as rector of All Saints' Church here because of his royalist sympathies, was the great, great grandfather of the first U.S. President, George Washington. The exquisite little parish church where Lawrence Washington served sits quietly at the top of a hill to this day.

Purleigh is a sleepy village clustered around the 13th-century church. On the road that leads to the church there is a delightful house called The Thatched Cottage, which has an unusual and intricate thatch design.

**Lawrence Washington, the "malignant royalist"**
"A malignant royalist who should be removed from the ministry." This was the description given the Reverend Lawrence Washington when opponents of the king ousted him from his church. Washington, who was thought by his parishioners to be "a very worthy and pious man," left in disgrace, never to return, and died penniless. Unhappy with the harsh and unjust treatment of their father, his

sons John and Lawrence left England to seek a fresh start in the New World.

Lawrence Washington was born at Sulgrave Manor, Oxfordshire, in 1602 and educated at Oxford. He was elected a fellow of the college in 1623, but he resigned his fellowship on his marriage to Amphyllis Twigden in 1633. He was appointed the rector of the beautiful little church at Purleigh in March of that year.

The future looked very promising for Washington and his new bride. Her family believed she had married well, as Washington was born of a wealthy and influential family and his prospects were good. It is believed that during their first year at Purleigh Amphyllis gave birth to their first child, John, after which were born Lawrence, Margaret and Martha. Lawrence already had two children, William and Elizabeth, from his first marriage.

These were difficult times in England. The English Civil War, the struggle between the royalist supporters of Charles I and the Parliamentarians (those who supported the Parliament), had begun in 1642. The royalists, known for their love of the finer things in life, wore beautiful plumed feather hats, velvet clothes, and high leather boots. Their cavalier mannerisms were infamous. The Puritan Parliamentarians, on the other hand, wore somber clothes and strove to behave in a virtuous and pious manner.

By all accounts, Washington was a good minister, but he was known to enjoy a drink or two at the local inn. His daily "tippling" was the focus of much discussion by the elders of the church, and the parliamentarians accused him of "... encouraging others in the same beastly vice."

The situation deteriorated, and in 1643 the Reverend Washington was branded a "malignant royalist" and banished from the rectory at Purleigh. This was seen as a diabolical act by the village folk. Henry Ayloffe, the justice of the peace, reflected the views of many when he wrote that the reverend "...always appeared a very sober, modest person. He was a loyal person and had one of the best benefices in these parts, and this was the only cause of his expulsion, as I verily believe."

After Washington was ousted from the ministry, he took his family briefly to Little Baxted, a small village, and then on to Maldon. In 1649 the Committee for Plundered Ministers, organized to help the clergy and their families in times of distress, decreed that John Rogers, Washington's appointed successor, should pay one-fifth of his annual income of £218 to Washington and his family. This paltry sum was barely enough to survive. In about 1652, Washington died in poverty at the age of 50 and was buried at All Saints' Church in Maldon, Essex.

Unhappy and disillusioned by their father's severe treatment at the hands of the Parliamentarians, John and his brother Lawrence decided to leave their homeland for the New World. John was the first to leave, around 1656 serving as a mate on the *Sea Horse* of London, a sailing vessel traveling to the colonies. He eventually settled in Virginia and married Anne Pope whose father gave John a 700-acre estate as a wedding gift. It was John Washington who was the great grandfather of George Washington, America's first President.

# What to see and do today:
## All Saints' Church
All Saints' Church sits on a hill enveloped in trees, half hidden from the world. The church, first constructed around 1220, was rebuilt in the fourteenth century. The influence of the Norman style (which arrived with William the Conqueror) can be seen in the church tower, with its knapped flintstone cladding and beautiful enameled blue clock face and gold numbering. A weather vane sits atop the church in the shape of a fish, an early emblem of Christianity.

The peaceful churchyard where Lawrence Washington must have once performed burials is now overgrown with grass. A gravel path leads to weather-beaten gravestones that barely give a clue as to who is buried beneath; some lie on their side, others on their backs facing the sky.

The interior of this tiny church, so small that the rector also serves as bell ringer and organist, is an unexpected pleasure. There are six carved pews on each side of the aisle, which is paved with black and red flagstones. The hexagonal pulpit decorated with fruit and foliage is quite unusual. Above the tower arch there is a partial royal coat of arms with a medallion painting of a youthful George III, giving an indication that it was finished soon after his accession to the throne in 1760.

## The Bells of Purleigh
It's comforting to think that four of the six bells at All Saints' Church were commissioned by Lawrence Washington. Lawrence reputedly had his own memorial cast made for the bells so he could proclaim his royalist allegiance each time they were rung. The famous Essex bell founder, Miles Gray of Colchester, supplied the bells in 1636. The inscription on the bells reads "Miles Gray Made Me

M1636." To mark the bells' tercentenary, the British Broadcasting Company broadcast the peal of the bells at Purleigh directly to the U.S. on July 5, 1936, to honor the village's connection to George Washington.

**The Church Vineyard**
This region has a long history of wine making. The first recorded vineyard in Purleigh dates to 1120. That vineyard was located close to the church and covered only three acres, but presumably it produced enough wine to keep the village folk satisfied. In 1163 the vineyard became the property of the Crown, and all the wine it produced was sent to London for the consumption of King Henry II and his court. It is recorded that in 1207, two "tuns" (barrels, about 360 bottles today) were sent to the town of Bury St. Edmunds to celebrate the arrival of King John.

**New Hall Vineyard**
Established in 1969, the New Hall vineyard boasts that it is the largest vineyard in East Anglia, producing over 200,000 bottles of wine each year. The vineyard has won scores of international awards for its wine, including over 30 gold medals. The selection of wine for sale varies in price but includes an award-winning dry sparkling wine and a unique pinot noir.
Open: 10:00 a.m. until 5:00 p.m. Monday to Friday and 10:00 a.m. until 1:30 p.m. on Saturday and Sunday. Telephone: (0) 1621 818343 – Mr. Greenwood. Address: Chelmsford Road, Purleigh.

# Food for thought:
**The Bell Inn**
The Bell Inn, which sits at the foot of the church, was built in the sixteenth century and is quite possibly the very inn that Lawrence Washington frequented for his

"tippling." The inn still serves as the main meeting place of the villagers. Exposed wooden beams and a roaring fire in the ancient stone fireplace create a wonderful atmosphere. Owners Barry and Julie Mott offer traditional pub fare and, of course, the local beer in plenty.
Open: 11:00 a.m. until 10:30 p.m. for lunch and dinner. Telephone: (0) 162 828348. Address: Next to All Saints' Church, Purleigh.

**The Queen's Head**
You will also find great food and a wide selection of beer at the Queen's Head, however it's only open at weekends. The building that houses the pub was constructed in 1784, and it originally served as a parish workhouse or "poorhouse" as they were known in their day. Commissioned by the Churchwardens and Overseers of the Poor, its residents were mainly widows and orphans. The workhouse history notes that 11 beds and 15 chairs were part of the inventory. Four spinning wheels served as "education" for the girls, and the boys were taught how to make shoes and other trades.
Open: Saturdays and Sundays only. Sue Hammond. Telephone: (0) 1621 828229. Address: Rudley Green, Chelmsford Road, Purleigh.

## If you decide to stay:
Although there are no accommodations in Purleigh, there are several good hotels in Maldon, about five miles to the east of the village, and at South Wooden Ferrers, about five miles south of Purleigh.

**Oakland Hotel**
The hotel has a large restaurant and caters for vegetarians and those with specific dietary needs. Special tours of the local sights including Colchester can be arranged through the hotel staff.

Telephone: (0) 1245 322811.  Address: 2-6 Reeves Way, South Woodham Ferrers, Chelmsford, Essex.

## How to get there:

There is direct train service from London to Chelmsford. From Chelmsford, there is bus service to Maldon, and local service from Maldon to Purleigh. As there is no train or bus service directly to Purleigh from London, the easiest way to get there is by car.

**By car**: Head northeast from London on the A12. You'll see signposts for Brentwood and Chelmsford. Be certain to bypass Chelmsford by staying on the A12 when it veers to the right just south of the city. Stay on the bypass for about four miles, and then take the A414 east toward Maldon. Continue on the A414 to Danbury, and at the roundabout take the B1010 to Purleigh. Purleigh is approximately 45 miles away from central London, about an hour's drive.

# Maldon

Maldon is a bustling town perched on a hill that combines ancient buildings and new shops in a manner to delight the visitor. Centuries-old homes painted in the pastel colors so typical of Essex and the red-sailed Thames barges moored at Hythe Quay provide a picturesque quality to a town steeped in history.

This busy town still owes much of its livelihood to the sea, as it has since ancient times. It sits on the river Blackwater, which discharges into the North Sea, thus giving ships traveling along the coastline of England direct access. During the Dark Ages this made the town vulnerable to attacks from Viking ships, and Maldon is the site of a famous battle in which villagers defended the town from Viking invaders.

Maldon is also the resting place of Lawrence Washington, ancestor of George Washington; he is buried at the delightful All Saints' Church, which has a spectacular stained-glass window commemorating his life.

Maldon was once known as "that jewel on the East Coast" because of the supposed healing powers of its densely salted estuaries. Over the years, farmers have reclaimed much of the marshland but if you look carefully, you may see what Daniel Defoe, the author of *Robinson Crusoe,* meant after a visit to the village. He wrote "...from the marshes and low ground, not being able to travel without many windings and indentures, by the reason of creeks and waters, I came to the town of Maldon."

**The Battle of Maldon**
Maldon's location on the river Blackwater and its rich and bountiful farms have always made the town vulnerable to those who came by sea to attack and plunder. The Battle of Maldon — in which a band of villagers armed with scythes defended their land from sea-faring warriors, led by a brave village elder who lost his life — came to be one of the most famous battles in Saxon history.

Excavations have shown that Maldon has been settled since the Bronze Age. The name of Maldon is thought to have derived from the Saxon *mael,* meaning "speech"' or a "place of meeting" and *dun,* meaning a "cross on a hilltop." In 916, the Saxon king Edward the Elder built a fort (or *burh*) at the head of the estuary to guard against marauding Vikings. Although it helped protect the town for many years, it proved no match for the Vikings when they finally came to conquer.

The Vikings were soldier-sailors and highly skilled oarsmen. Their callused hands allowed them to row for long periods without fatigue. The rhythmic pull of 16 or more professional warriors on each side of the boat allowed them to stealthily approach a village and then attack, loot, and withdraw without loss of men. While traveling, their wooden shields hung on the outside of the boat like badges of victory. When they attacked, they wore chain mail, battered conical steel helmets and wielded terrifying iron axes that were capable of inflicting mortal wounds.

It was Britnoth, an Anglo-Saxon leader of Essex, who rallied the villagers to defend their town. He was a wealthy man and the largest landowner in Essex. He was impressive in stature, standing over six feet tall, with a shock of long white hair that touched his shoulders. At a meeting between the Viking leader and Britnoth, the Viking demanded gold, cattle and other valuables, and insinuated that the Saxons had no stomach for battle. The insult infuriated Britnoth, and so the fighting began.

Legend has it that the Viking leader pleaded with Britnoth in the name of fair play to allow him to reassemble his troops after they were stranded in mud on the banks of the Blackwater. Britnoth gave his word for them to do so, but this proved to be a terrible strategic move. After he realized his mistake, Britnoth would not go back on his word. He died that day along with many of his men. Although the villagers fought bravely, they were no match for the experienced warriors. After the battle, the remaining villagers returned to the scene and collected the headless body of Britnoth and buried him. Some sources state that Britnoth's skull crossed the North Sea with the Vikings, who eventually used it as a drinking vessel.

## What to see and do today:
### All Saints' Church
The magnificent All Saints' Church, which dates from the 12th century, was built on a previous Saxon church site. It is easiest to appreciate the church by looking at it from across the road at the junction of Silver and High Streets. The unique triangular tower supports a shingled hexagon-shaped spire. In the nineteenth century, statues of five of the most important people of the area were added to the buttresses of the church, including St. Cedd, Britnoth, and Thomas Plume.

There is a splendid stained-glass window on the church's south wall that honors Lawrence Washington, the great, great grandfather of George Washington. Washington arrived with his family in 1643 after being ousted from his position as rector of the church in Purleigh. He lived in Maldon on a pittance with his wife and six children until his death in 1652. He is buried in the churchyard, but the actual site of his grave is not known. The window was a gift from the citizens of Malden, Massachusetts, in 1928 to commemorate Lawrence Washington's life.

**Thomas Plume's Library**
Thomas Plume's library has been called Maldon's treasure. Plume was born in Maldon in 1630. He rose to the position of archdeacon in Rochester, Kent, where he died in 1704. Upon his death, he bequeathed his substantial library to the town of Maldon and neighboring villages so "…that a Gentleman or Scholar who desires may go into it and make use of any book there or borrow it."
Open: The library is run by volunteers and visiting hours vary. Call for details.
Telephone: (0) 1621 854051. Address: On the top floor of the Maeldune Heritage Center, which is located at the top of Market Hill, Maldon.

**Maldon District Museum**
This charming museum offers an eclectic range of displays, from a mummified lady's hand to a penny-farthing bicycle (a bicycle whose large front wheel and much smaller rear wheel are reminiscent of the large old English penny and much smaller farthing). You will also find Roman, Anglo–Saxon, Viking, and medieval artifacts. There is also a wonderful portrait of Horatio Gates, a Maldon man who started his military career as a British officer and later became an American general in the War of Independence.
Open: Wednesday, Thursday and Friday from 2:00 p.m. until 4:00 p.m.; Saturday and Sunday from 2:00 p.m. until 5:00 p.m. The museum is run by volunteers so it's a good idea to call ahead for opening times.
Telephone: (0) 1621 842688. Address: 47 Mill Road, Maldon.

**Hythe Quay**
Hythe Quay is home to many boats and ships, including the famous red-sailed Thames barges. The quay holds an important place in the town's development and history. For centuries, barges have ferried the town's chief exports — wheat, cheese, butter, oats, timber, leather goods and crystal salt — from the quay. Most of the goods were shipped to London but the barges often stopped at other destinations along the way.
Today Hythe Quay attracts many visitors and residents who enjoy the sights and sounds of the river. The quay is a photographer's paradise, offering everything from the graceful lines of ships' rigging to busy and colorful marsh birds.

**The Maldon Salt Company**
The process of salt making has been an Essex specialty for over 2,000 years. Essex has some of the saltiest estuaries

in Britain because the sea water pools in the narrow inlets around the coastline. In ancient times the sea water was collected in clay pots and heated until the water evaporated, leaving only the salt crystals behind. The same basic process is used today, except that stainless steel vats have replaced the clay pots. The Domesday Book mentions 45 salt pans in and around the Maldon area, an indication of the value placed on salt production since the Middle Ages.

## Food for thought:
### The Queen's Head and The Jolly Sailor Pubs
Both pubs overlook Hythe Quay. They each serve the traditional pub food with a good variety of beer and atmosphere. The Jolly Sailor is approximately 400 years old and has 4 guest bedrooms available for visitors.
Telephone: (0) 1621 853463. Address: Hythe Quay.

## If you decide to stay:
### The Blue Boar
The Blue Boar is Maldon's oldest inn. It has been a coaching hotel since the 15th century and has some of the finest examples of centuries' old exposed wall and ceiling timbers in the town. In the coach yard at the rear of the inn, there are magnificent half-timbered buildings with overhanging upper stories that appear to be toppling into the yard.
Telephone: (0) 1621 852681. Address: Silver Street across the road from All Saints' Church.

### The Swan Hotel
The Swan Hotel is a 14th-century building with some of the charming original features. Special diets are catered for and children are welcome. Tea and coffee appliances are in each bedroom for the convenience of guests.

Telephone (0) 1621 853170. Address: 73 High Street, Maldon.

## Neighboring places of interest:
### Bradwell-on-Sea
Saint Cedd was a Northumbrian monk who belonged to the famed Lindisfarne monastery in Ireland. Cedd was sent as a missionary to the pagan East Saxons at the behest of their king after he converted to Christianity. Cedd was quite successful, building churches in Lastingham in Yorkshire and Prittlewell in Essex. Cedd then set his sights on the eastern coast of England.

Cedd built the chapel of St. Peter-on-the-Wall in about 645. It is believed to sit on the site of Othona, a Roman fort, one of a number built along the Saxon shore to protect against marauding Saxons. The church is built of reused Roman materials and Kentish ragstone. Because so much of the building remains standing, it is considered by some to be the oldest church in England. There is a pilgrimage each year to this mysterious chapel on the first Saturday in July.

## For more information:
Maldon has a great tourist information center.
Telephone: (0) 621-856503. Address: Coach Lane, Maldon. Open: Daily 10:00 a.m. until 4:00 p.m. Year round. (October through March, Saturdays only: 10:00 a.m. until 1:30 p.m.)

## How to get there:
There is direct train service from London to Chelmsford, from where the visitor may take a local bus to Maldon. As there is no direct train service from London, the easiest way to get to Maldon is by car.

**By car**: Head northeast from London on the A12. You'll see signposts for Brentwood and Chelmsford. Be certain to bypass Chelmsford by staying on the A12 when it veers to the right just south of the city. Stay on the bypass for about four miles, and then take the A414 east toward Maldon. Continue on the A414 to Danbury, and at the roundabout take the B1010 to Purleigh. Follow the signs to the town center, where you'll find a great "pay-and-display" parking lot. Maldon is about 50 miles away from central London, and the drive will take about 90 minutes.

To reach Bradwell-on-Sea, take B1018 south from Maldon. After about four miles, B1018 takes a sharp left turn and goes due east through Latchingdon to a junction with B1021 at Southminster. Follow B1021 north to Bradwell. Once in the village, look for East End Road, which is opposite the pub, and take it toward Sales Point until you see a sign for St. Cedd's in a parking lot next to a farm cottage. Be prepared for a half-mile walk to the chapel on a gravel footpath carved through a cornfield.
Services: Sunday Evensong, July – August, 6:30 p.m.
Telephone: (0) 621 856503. Maldon Tourist Board for more information.

# Dedham

The Domesday Book reports that in 1086, Dedham had a population of over two hundred people and various livestock. The book was prepared by William the Conqueror after his invasion of England in 1066. His scribes were sent into the countryside to assess the population and livestock of each village so a tax could be levied against all the wealth in the land. So feared were the Britons of this inventory, they named the book after God's final Day of Judgment.

Dedham is a delightful village. The name probably originated from the Saxon, *Dydda's Ham*, or possibly the name of an original family called Dydda. Dedham lay on a main road later to be known as The King's Highway that linked Colchester and Ipswich. There are three ancient tracks in the village: Pound Lane, Manningtree Path and Pig Lane. Later, Pig Lane would become East Lane during the reign of Queen Victoria.

Dedham and the surrounding towns are known as Constable Country after John Constable, the famous landscape painter. His beautiful paintings depicting the country scenes he loved so much adorn museums around the world.

John Constable so cherished this countryside that he wrote, "I love every stile and stump and lane...these scenes made me a painter and I am grateful...I had often thought of pictures of them before I ever touched a pencil."

The son of a prosperous corn merchant, Constable was born in 1776 in East Bergholt, Suffolk, just across the border of Essex. His parents owned two mills; one at Flatford, the subject of one of his popular paintings and the other at Dedham. He attended the Grammar School in Dedham under the strict direction of Dr. Grimwood who was the Headmaster at the time. He was a good student by all accounts but prone to dreaming. His intellectual ability was expected to bring him a position in the church, but his love of sketching and painting everyday scenes took him in a different direction. Often he would take his father's barge from the mill along the stream directly to school. We know from comments he made later that he noticed everything, "no two days are alike, not even two hours; neither were there ever two leaves of a tree alike since the creation of the world."

In 1799, when he was twenty-three year old, Constable was accepted as a probationer in the Royal Academy Schools in London. His work was not considered particularly interesting but when he began his "six footers," most notably *The White Horse,* a biographer remarked that Constable "was too large to remain unnoticed."

At the age of thirty, Constable met Maria Bicknell, a local girl and granddaughter of the Rector at East Bergholt. He asked for her hand in marriage, but the Rector was against the union so the couple was confined to clandestine meetings and letters. They finally married some eighteen years later after a long and arduous engagement. They had seven children together and when Maria died in 1828, Constable's most productive years in painting ended.

# What to see and do today:
## St. Mary the Virgin
The Parish Church of St. Mary the Virgin was built in 1492 and has witnessed many changes over the centuries. During the reign of King Henry VIII and the Reformation, many stained-glass windows were destroyed. St. Mary the Virgin was no exception. However, one tiny piece of stained glass survived at St. Mary. It is known as the Sherman Glass and can be seen above the Webbe tomb. The glass still bears the initials E.S. for Edmund Sherman, whose ancestors played an important part in the development of America. On Edmund Sherman's death in 1600, he left his house to the Governors of the Free Grammar School of Queen Elizabeth for a school to teach boys to "read, write and cast accounts."

In 1967 the people of Dedham, Massachusetts helped with the renovations of the church by donating one thousand pounds (sterling). Their generosity is remembered with a beautifully carved pew at the West End of the church.

## The Sherman Home
Located across the road from St. Mary the Virgin church sits the Sherman home. It is in good condition and still in use even today. At least six of the Sherman children emigrated to the United States of America between 1633 and 1640. They became the co-founders of Rhode Island, signatories of the Declaration of Independence, as well as becoming other notable dignitaries.

## River Walks
There are various notable walks through Constable Country starting in Dedham village. They range from 3 to almost 5 miles. These walks meander through Dedham and Flatford Mills and on to Langham Church. There are pamphlets available in the Countryside Center depicting these

walks. "As Constable Saw It" is a wonderful pamphlet showing twelve of Constable's sketches dated between 1796 and 1832. It is interesting to see how little the countryside has changed during the last two hundred years.

**The River Stour**
The River Stour, so often depicted in Constable's paintings, is the natural boundary between Essex and Suffolk. It has meandered around the countryside transporting agricultural produce, fuel, wool and timber in flat bottom barges for centuries. No longer used for commercial traffic, it is used only for boating and fishing when the season allows. A variety of fish can be found in the Stour including perch, pike, gudgeon, minnows and eels.

A walk along this beautiful river will provide wonderful opportunities to see the abundant birds, trees and flowers Constable loved to paint. Water lilies, watermint and bulrushes are host to kingfishers, swans and moorhens.

## Food for thought:
**The Marlborough Head**
The Marlborough Head is an early-15th-century coaching inn serving traditional English meals with charm and character galore. This inn is included in "the best 500 pubs list." The inn also has three guest bedrooms available, but remember to book early.
Telephone: (0) 1206 323124. Address: Mill Street, Dedham (opposite the church).

**The Essex Rose Tea Room**
Located across the road from the Marlborough, the Essex Rose Tea Room is a 16th-century building offering an excellent place for morning coffee, light lunch or afternoon Cream Tea. It has all the grace and charm of bygone times and wonderful food as well.

## If you decide to stay:
### Maison Talbooth Guest House
The Maison Talbooth guest house is a Victorian hotel offering a wonderful selection of services and amenities for visitors. The main meals are served in a 16$^{th}$-century restaurant on the banks, offering a fantastic view of the river Stour. They cater for vegetarian and special diet meals, and also feature a fully licensed bar.
Telephone: (0) 1206 322367. Address: Stratford Road, Dedham.

## For more information:
Telephone: (0) 1206 282920. Tourist Information Center, Colchester.

## Neighboring places of interest:
**Manningtree**, about three miles east of Dedham is a quiet and delightful riverside town, known as the smallest parish in Essex. It is notorious for being the birthplace of Matthew Hopkins, a Manningtree lawyer who was later known as the "Witchfinder General." He assumed the ominous title because of his ability to find witches. He was paid twenty shillings by Parliament for every town he visited and soon gained a reputation for "persuading" witches to confess. The business became so lucrative that he formed his own close-knit crew to comb the countryside seeking out witches of both genders. At one time, he had 32 people under arrest of whom 19 were hanged in one day.

At the end of his career, Hopkins' techniques came to the attention of Parliament who demanded an explanation for his cruel antics. Hopkins submitted a pamphlet to Parliament in 1647 defending his actions and techniques. During Hopkins' reign of terror, almost four hundred men and

*The Dedham Sign*

women from local villages and towns had been condemned to death, sometimes for merely owning a cat! Matthew Hopkins is buried in Mistley Towers, a little village east of Manningtree.

## How to get there:
There is direct train service from London to Manningtree, from where Dedham can be reached by taxi. As there is no train or bus service directly to Dedham from London, the easiest way to get there is by car.

**By car**: Head northeast from London on the A12. You'll see signposts for Brentwood and Chelmsford. Stay on the A12 for about 44 miles, using the bypasses to go around Chelmsford and Colchester. Look for the exit for Park Lane, which is about 3 miles after the junction of the A12 and A120. Take this exit to Wick Road and turn right. Turn right at the next junction, Birchwood Road, and go on to Grove Hill, and then on into Dedham. Dedham is approximately 63 miles away from central London.

# St. Osyth

Frithewald, King of the East Angles and first Christian ruler of his tribe, was in constant fear of being attacked by marauding Danes, whose notoriety preceded them. They were known for their brutal attacks, sparing no life regardless of age or gender. He and his wife Wilaburga were fearful that their home would be pillaged and their beautiful young daughter, Osyth, would be kidnapped.

Frithewald and Wilaburga were so concerned for Osyth's safety that they sent her away to the relative security of the county of Warwickshire. Her personal care and spiritual guidance were placed in the hands of Abbess St. Moden, who ran a strict priory but provided love and care of her novices.

One day, Abbess St. Moden sent young Osyth on an important mission. It was to visit a nearby priory to collect a precious book from the Abbess St. Edith, sister of King Alfred. Osyth set off immediately, pleased that she had been given such a significant task. After her visit to the neighboring priory, Osyth carefully carried away the book, mindful of her duties to guard its safety. However, on her return journey, the weather worsened and as she crossed a bridge, she was swept into the swollen torrents of the fast-moving river.

Three days passed without St. Moden hearing from Osyth so she decided to visit St. Edith herself. St. Edith told the

Abbess that Osyth had collected the book as instructed and, after some brief refreshment, had set off on her return trip that same day. Prior to knowing that Osyth was missing, St. Edith had a vision in which an angel told her to visit the river. Believing this to be an omen, the two women set out on their journey fearing the worst, but they found Osyth sitting quietly by the river with the precious book unharmed in her hands.

Another legend concerns Osyth's adult life. When she became a grown woman, her parents betrothed her to Sighere, King of the East Saxons, or Essex, as it is known today. She was an obedient girl and would not defy their wishes and so agreed to marry Sighere. On the morning of the wedding, Osyth's father, the groom and the men of the wedding party noticed a white deer in a clearing of the woods. They took off in pursuit of the deer, leaving Osyth and the womenfolk alone. As she sat quietly awaiting her fate, Osyth decided the life of a nun was preferable to becoming Queen of the East Saxons and she defied her parents' wishes and stole quietly away to a nearby convent where she quickly "took the veil." Sighere was devastated when he returned from the hunt, but he loved her deeply and only wanted her happiness. Sighere's love for Osyth was so great that he built a priory for her on a quiet inlet on the coast. It was not long before she was administering to several young novices of her own and pursuing her dream of serving Christ.

In 653, on a warm summer's day, a band of Viking pirates led by Hubba and Inguar swept into the village and came upon Osyth's convent. The Vikings terrorized the nuns but Osyth stood her ground and proclaimed her faith in God. The Viking Hubba ordered Osyth to recant her faith and accept their pagan god. She would not, which infuriated the Viking, who ordered a warrior to severe her head. The order was carried out and according to local legend, after Osyth had been decapitated she gently bent down, picked up her head and walked to the chapel. Once at the chapel door, her bloodied hand pushed it open and she fell dead upon the floor.

## What to see and do today:
### The Village
The village and port of St. Osyth was granted a charter in 1215 giving grants, special rights and exemptions. Any stone that was needed to expand the priory probably came by barges along the causeway. The bargemen also plied their trade, taking grain and straw to London and returning with manure from the stables to fertilize the fields. It is easy to see how vulnerable St. Osyth was to attack as the causeway gives direct access from the open sea.

The cottages on Mill Street date back to the 15th and 16th centuries and show excellent examples of Essex weatherboard. Sometimes this kind of exterior finish on cottages is called shiplap, where boards are rabbeted so the edges of each board lap over the next.

### St. Osyth's Priory
The Priory is a beautiful, romantic building with magnificent grounds extending over 250 acres. It is believed to have been built on the previous grounds of St. Osyth's priory. Sections date to the eleventh century and the splendid medieval gateway is said to be the finest England. The external walls are of knapped flint, and spiral chimneys adorn some of the buildings. These were obviously added at a much later date but they do not detract from the beauty of this extraordinary structure.

Unfortunately, the priory is closed to the public at the present time. However, discussions are under way to open for visitors in the near future.
Telephone: (0) 1255 423400 Clacton-on-Sea Tourist Center.

**St. Peter and St. Paul's Church**
St. Peter and St. Paul's is a handsome church in an idyllic setting. A stained-glass window depicts a Saxon church and the legend of St. Osyth. Records of the village history suggest there was a similar window in the church that was built around 1120. The ceiling of the north aisle is beautifully and intricately carved. Initially the church was quite large but in 1549 when King Henry VIII dissolved the monasteries, it was demolished leaving only the small, parish church we see today.

**St. Clere's Hall**
St. Clere's Hall was once the 14$^{th}$-century home of the wealthy and influential D'Arcy family. In 1582, Brian D'Arcy, Justice of the Peace in St. Osyth, conducted searches for witches in the village and neighboring areas. He used the same persuasive techniques as Matthew Hopkins of Manningtree, Essex, who had the ominous title of Witchfinder General. A book in the Bodleian Library, Oxford, states that, "A true and just recorde of the enformation, examination and confession of all witches taken at St. Osees." The evidence consisted of accusations by neighbors and even family members of supposed witchcraft. Two local women, Elizabeth Bennet and Ursula Kemp, were branded as witches. Ursula's own son, Thomas, gave evidence against his mother at the trial. The two women were found guilty and hanged for witchcraft in 1582.

*St. Osyth's Priory*

In 1921, a man digging in his garden at 37 Mill Street came upon two skeletons. The main joints of the women were bound, elbow to elbow, wrist to wrist. The skeletons are believed to be the remains of Elizabeth and Ursula, and we can only assume that they were bound together to prevent them escaping their joint grave.

During the Civil War, around 1645, another twenty-two women were accused and tried for witchcraft. Twelve were hanged, two died in prison and one died on the way to the scaffold. There is no record of what happened to the remaining seven witches.

Queen Elizabeth I encouraged the seeking out of witches. She stayed at the priory in 1561 and again in 1579 in the company of Lord John D'Arcy, whose tomb is in the church.

Very little remains of St. Cleres Hall today but there were always rumors about a secret passage leading from the house to the priory. Then, during WWII, a tunnel was discovered and excavations were made to determine where the tunnel began and ended. It is believed that it ran between St. Cleres Hall and the Priory and was approximately 900 yards.

### Legends of St.Osyth
Every village as old as St. Osyth has its share of legends. The earliest is of a fiery dragon that moved through the village in 1189 so quickly that it left buildings smoldering. A ghostly mail coach pulled by six horses has supposedly been followed from the Flag Inn towards Wheeley and a ghostly woman in white clothes is often seen. Such are the phantoms in St. Osyth.

## Food for thought:
**The Priory Restaurant** is considered by the locals as a good place to eat. The bread is baked daily and they offer a wonderful selection of cooked meats and cheeses. A scrumptious Cream Tea is also available in the afternoon. Telephone: (0) 1255 820259. Address: Clacton Road, St. Osyth. (Next to the Red Lion Pub).

## A place to stay:
**The Red Lion** has rooms with bathrooms en suite. They offer the traditional pub food and a great bar with cask-conditioned beers to enjoy in their beer garden.
Telephone: (0) 1255 820256. Address: Clacton Road, St. Osyth.

## Neighboring places of interest:
There are several towns north of St. Osyth worthy of a visit. **Clacton-on-Sea** is a very busy seaside town, with shops, pubs and tourists. It is a well-known Edwardian seaside resort and only 10 minutes drive away from St.

Osyth. There is an action-packed pier and great seaside pubs along the esplanade.

A couple of miles north of Clacton is **Frinton-on-Sea**, a well-established seaside resort. It is smaller and less busy than Clacton, and also has the advantage of a great walk along the promenade to Walton-on-the-Naze, the neighboring town to the north.

## How to get there:
There is direct train service from London's Liverpool Street station to Clacton-on-Sea from where St. Osyth can be reached by taxi.

**By car:** Head northeast from London on the A12. You'll see signposts for Brentwood and Chelmsford. Be certain to bypass Chelmsford by staying on the A12 when it veers to the right just south of the city. Stay on the A12 all the way to Colchester. Just outside Colchester look for the junction with A133. Turn east onto the A133 and head towards Clacton-on-Sea. Continue into the outskirts of Clacton to the roundabout junction with B1027. Turn right (west) onto B1027 and travel about 2 miles to St. Osyth. St. Osyth is about 75 miles away from central London.

# Coggeshall

It was called the "Coggeshall Whites" and was said to be the finest cloth in the world. Sought by the clergy in Portugal, Spain and the noblemen of Europe, it was the beginning of Coggeshall's wealth in the 15th century, a legacy still seen today in the opulent buildings in the village. The Grange Barn built by the Cistercian monks in 1145 is part of that legacy and is considered to be the oldest building of its type in Europe.

Archaeological studies have shown the remnants of a Roman settlement at Coggeshall. This is hardly surprising since the town is only seven miles east of Colchester, Britain's oldest recorded Roman town. The village is located on the old Roman road that connects Colchester to St. Albans and then continues west through the town of Bishop's Stortford.

In 1145, an order of Benedictine monks arrived from France, bringing with them their skills of brick making, brewing and tanning. The monks were also skilled farmers whose crops flourished in the arable soil of Essex. They also specialized in sheep breeding, and it is believed their expertise in cross breeding resulting in the fine wool cloth that was eventually known as the Coggeshall Whites.

The name Coggeshall can be traced back to Sir Thomas Coggeshall, knight of the realm, who lived in the village during the reign of King Stephen and Queen Matilda from approximately 1135 until 1154. Centuries later in 1576, one of Thomas' descendants, John Coggeshall, and the village were granted a crest. The crest has a red cross in the center dividing it into four sections. Each section contains a symbol depicting items of important local life: a sheath of wheat, a sheep, a cockerel and two crossed keys.

In the middle of the 15th century, John Paycocke arrived from Clare, Suffolk. There are few historical facts known about the family, but judging from church records and the will left by Thomas Paycocke to the people in the village, they were kind and considerate. The beautiful house built by the Paycocke family still stands as a testament to the excellent workmanship of the day. This charming and ornate home reflects the opulent times when a man of means could indulge himself. The front of the home is adorned with a band of exquisite carvings of flowers, leaves, Tudor roses, a King and Queen and cherub-like children. The initials of Thomas and Margaret Coggeshall are carved in the beams around the house; such was their love for each other.

During the 15th century, the village quickly grew in size and soon became one of the most prominent in Essex. At this time, looms could be heard clacking from morning until night in almost every cottage. This was the beginning of the "outwork" system, indicating the work was done at home. Later the same work would be completed in workhouses for the poor, mostly by women and children. Finally, the workhouses gave way to factories and mass production.

The Paycocke family took full advantage of the Dutch refugees fleeing the religious persecution in their own country for a better life in England. The Flemish weavers were fine craftsmen, experts in the cloth making process. The combination of their skill and the high quality of wool were the foundation of Coggeshall's prosperity and the development of the beautiful, half-timbered homes we still see today, including the large 15th-century cathedral-style church of St. Peter-ad-Vincula.

Over the years, the increase in wealth from the wool trade brought the inevitable taxes and duties, which encouraged groups of smugglers to spring up all over Essex. The Essex rivers such as the Blackwater and Crouch open directly to the North Sea and, therefore, were havens for smugglers who played a deadly game of cat and mouse with the Customs men. With skill and knowledge of the area, the smugglers would constantly outwit the Customs men in their fast-sailing cutters.

Another name for a smuggler was "owler." The name may have originated with the nocturnal activities they performed or possibly even the call itself. The fear among smugglers of a traitor in their midst was so great that an "owling fraternity"' was established with their own rules and punishment.

The Crown considered the wool trade so important to England's prosperity that a penalty of death was imposed for outward smuggling. To this day, the Lord Chancellor in the House of Lords sits on a large "wool sack" as a reminder that England earned its wealth from the wool trade.

Long after the demise of the wool trade in Coggeshall, a series of crimes plagued the village from 1844 through 1848. The Coggeshall Gang was responsible for terrorizing the villagers into revealing the whereabouts of their valuables. However, the gang seemed more interested in wine, food and candles. They operated mostly at night, masked and armed with pistols and cudgels. One gang member named William Wade was arrested and transported to the

Colonies for fifteen years. Wade agreed not to divulge the identity of the gang leader, Samuel Crow, or other members of the gang if they would provide for his wife and family. The gang failed to honor their commitment so Wade informed the authorities of the members' identities and their headquarters at the Black Horse Inn, in Stonegate Street. The proprietor of the inn, William French, was the gang leader's half brother. No doubt French took advantage of the gang's spoils and passed them through his own establishment.

Samuel Crow escaped the hands of the law and made his way to London. There he purchased a ticket for Hamburg on the steamer *James Watt*. Unfortunately for Crow, policeman James Puddifoot was on his trail. Puddifoot, having studied Crow's picture in the latest police brochure "Hue and Cry," recognized Crow as he boarded the ship and arrested him.

On the first Monday in March of 1848, the gang was brought to trial at Essex Lent Assizes in Chelmsford. Details in the Chelmsford Chronicle note that the galleries were "filled to suffocation by respectfully dressed females." William Wade saved himself from a death sentence by testifying against the other members of the gang. The jury took only twelve minutes to reach the verdict of guilty. The punishment varied in consideration of involvement in the crimes but Crow and two other members of the gang were transported to the Colonies for life.

Samuel Crow never served his sentence but died in Chelmsford prison in 1850. Wade had his sentence reduced to transportation for seven years in the Colonies and so ended the regime of terror by the Coggeshall Gang.

**Legends and Ley Lines**
There are many mysteries in and around the village such as the black cat that was bricked into a wall or that hooded figures used to attend funerals at night carrying flaming torches. On February 15, 1555, a local man, Thomas Hawkes, died by fire rather than have his child baptized in the Roman Catholic Church. Legend has it that during his final minutes, he raised his hands above his head and clapped three times proclaiming his faith in God and defying his tormentors' demands.

Some believe the village has strange powers because it sits upon crossed Ley Lines. There are many theories regarding leys and their powers. Villages and churches are often found on ley lines, which usually run in a straight line over a hill, rather than round it. Some believe leys were an ancient surveying system giving travelers directions to sacred sites by using landmarks. A large stone (Markstone), a pile of stones (Cairn) or even a special group of trees would be used as a marker. The flow of energy along a ley has been studied for many years with some interesting results, although nothing is conclusive. Pilots have used ley lines for years as a means of orientation but others have tried to unravel the mystery by using aerial photographs, dowsing for magnetic forces and "subconscious sitting" in an attempt to feel the source of energy. Some believe that UFOs have flown in the direct path of leys sensing a magnetic field. These are interesting theories regarding the leys and legends of Coggeshall. The residents do not appear to be concerned and, more often than not, seem to be amused by them.

## What to see and do today:
Coggeshall is a quiet, unspoiled village offering a day of exploration and discovery. Local historians can arrange walking tours of the village and the main buildings of in-

terest but the wonderful little antique shops; specialty shops and pubs should not be ignored.

**The Grange Barn**
The Grange Barn built by the Cistercian monks in 1145 is considered to be the oldest surviving timber-framed barn in Europe. It is all that remains of the Abbey after the dissolution of the Abbeys by King Henry VIII around 1538. The chapel, guest house and abbots' lodge are now in private hands although they may sometimes be viewed by appointment.
Open: 2:00 p.m. until 5:00 p.m. Tuesday, Thursday and Sundays from April 2 through September 30. To arrange a personal guide of the village, please call (0) 1376 563003 (or 562855).

**Paycocke's Home**
The Paycocke's home is a beautiful half-timbered 15th-century house showing the opulence of the time. The wealth of the wool merchants is reflected in their homes and also the churches that were often (and still) called "wool" churches.
Open: 2:00 p.m. until 5:00 p.m. Tuesday, Thursday and Sundays from April 2 through September 30. To arrange a personal guide of the village, please call (0) 1376 563003 (or 562855).

**St. Peter ad Vincula**
The Parish Church was dedicated to St. Peter ad Vincula and was built using materials from local Roman buildings no later than 1105. The church was completely rebuilt in the 15th century in the cathedral style of the Wool Towns of the eastern counties.

**The Town Clock**
The current Town Clock was rebuilt on the site of an earlier clock tower to celebrate Queen Victoria's Jubilee in 1887. The Clockhouse was at one time "Hitcham School" for the poor children of the town.

## For more information:
Coggeshall Heritage Center
Telephone: 01376 563003. Address: St. Peter's Hall, Stoneham Street, Coggeshall.

## Food for thought:
**The Wool Pack Pub**
The Wool Pack Pub was originally a 15th-century coaching inn. Today it is known for its traditional English food, but the atmosphere is considered the best in the area. There are exposed oak beams throughout, and wonderful large open fireplaces.
Telephone: (0) 1376 561235. Address: 91 Church Street, Coggeshall.

*The Woolpack Pub*

A great place for morning coffee or wonderful afternoon Cream Teas. Located close to the antique and specialty shops in the village.
Telephone: (0) 1376 563242. Address: 1 Stoneham Street, Coggeshall.

## If you decide to stay:
### Woodlands Manor Hotel
The hotel is located about 7 miles west of Coggeshall and is a family-run establishment. The house was built in the 17th century and sits on approximately 6 acres with trees, gardens and a lake. There is a restaurant and a bar. Special consideration is given to children under three years of age; they can stay and eat for free.
Telephone: (0) 1245 361502. Address: Upper London Road, Black Notley, Braintree, Essex.

## How to get there:
There is direct train service from London's Liverpool Street station to Kelvedon, from where you can take a taxi to Coggeshall. However, the easiest way to get there is by car.

**By car**: Head northeast from London on the A12. You'll see signposts for Brentwood and Chelmsford. Be certain to bypass Chelmsford by staying on the A12 when it veers to the right just south of the city. Stay on the A12 all the way to the Mark's Tey junction about 3 miles east of Colchester. Take the A120 heading west directly into Coggeshall.

# Colchester

Boadicea, Queen of the Iceni tribe, reigned over the counties we now call Norfolk and Suffolk with her husband Prasutagus from approximately AD 48 to AD 60. She was a fine woman by all accounts, standing as tall as a man — with a booming voice that could not be ignored. The Greek, Dio Cassius, described her as "a Briton woman of the royal family" and of having a mass of red locks "the tawniest hair" that hung to her waist.

For many years the Romans tried to conquer the ancient Britons, who continually fought back and denied their attackers. The women fought alongside the men and earned a reputation for their spirit and bravery in battle. A Roman, Diodorus Siculos, wrote that the Celts' women were "nearly as tall as the men, whom they rival in courage."

During the year AD 43, the Emperor Claudius sent approximately sixty thousand troops to finally contain the Britons. There were many battles between the Romans and the various tribes of the area but the Iceni made peace with the Romans. Prasutagus was permitted to keep his kingdom, which he ruled under the discipline of Rome. During the following years, he and Boadicea had two daughters whom they loved dearly and life was peaceful until the death of Prasutagus in AD 60.

On the eve of his death, Prasutagus wrote a will stating that half his kingdom would be left to his wife and daughters. The other half would revert to Rome. Boadicea would be the beneficiary of her daughters' inheritance until they came of age or when they married, in which case it would be used as a dowry.

The Romans saw Prasutagus' death as an opportunity to seize the kingdom and wealth that had accumulated during his long and successful reign. They decided to accuse Prasutagus' estate of delinquent taxes that were due immediately. Boadicea challenged the claim of overdue taxes and, unable to justify the accusations, the Romans knew their scheme had failed leaving only one option. They instructed their soldiers to remove Boadicea by force, to crush and humiliate her and diminish her power.

Records of the time tell us that Boadicea was taken from her home and publicly flogged. The noblemen and women were heartbroken as they watched in horror at the treatment of their Queen. The shame was almost too much for Boadicea to bear, but the final blow came when her teenage daughters were taken from her and brutally ravaged by the Roman soldiers.

Believing their duty was done, the Roman soldiers left Boadicea's home but this was just the beginning of one of the bloodiest episodes in England's history. Queen Boadicea felt such fury and humiliation that she swore revenge on Rome and the Roman people.

Boadicea collected an army of over one hundred thousand people from various tribes that had never surrendered to the Romans and who now joined forces with the Iceni Queen. They each wore their tribe's tartan and painted their faces with woad, a blue substance derived from herbs and thought to instill fear in their adversaries. The Britons' custom of pounding drums, screaming at their enemies and undisciplined behavior was in stark comparison to the Romans who were known for their well-organized and strategic formations in battle.

First, Boadicea set her sights on Colchester, the foremost Roman city in England. The 9th Legion of the Roman army was guarding Colchester but they were no match for Boadicea and her soldiers. The city was quickly burned to the ground. News of Boadicea's success spread through Britain and many people, sensing victory over the Romans, joined the fight. It is believed that Boadicea's army totaled over 200,000 men and women at the final battle.

Boadicea's next target was London. In anticipation of her arrival, the city was almost deserted but she kept her promise and pillaged and burned the town until nothing was left.

After the victories in Colchester and London, Boadicea and her army marched home full of triumph and accomplishment. They were greeted with cheers and happiness for ending the oppressive rule of Rome.

It is said that over seventy thousand Roman soldiers died at the hands of Boadicea's army and that the Romans were ashamed and disgraced that a woman could inflict such devastation. This was the worst rebellion by the native tribes for seventeen years and the Senate decided to use their best and most aggressive troops to contain the uprising. A deadly force was needed to crush the Iceni Queen, and so word was sent to Suetonius Paulinus in Anglesey, Wales. Paulinus commanded the 14th and 20th Legions, who were known to be particularly fierce and combative. The legions had been fighting the Druids for control of Wales but now turned their attention south towards Boadicea's army.

The actual location of the final battle site between the Roman legions and Boadicea is unknown but according to Tacitus, a Roman historian, Boadicea appeared "tired and injured, in her clan tartan and armed to the teeth...in appearance, almost terrifying." Some say she was captured and died from poison taken by her own hand. Others say she died in prison from wounds inflicted during the battle. Either of these would have been preferable to being taken to Rome and subjected to harsh treatment or even execution in the gladiatorial arena.

On Victoria Embankment, near Westminster Bridge, in London there is a bronze statue of Boadicea and her two daughters on a scythe-wheeled chariot holding their javelins aloft ready for battle. This is a wonderful tribute to a brave and fearless woman who died for her beliefs and love of her family and country.

## What to see and do today:
### The Town of Colchester
The Romans defeated 11 British kings who submitted to Emperor Claudius in AD 43. By doing so, Colchester became the first Roman Capital of Britain. After Queen Boadicea burned the town to the ground in AD 60, the Romans built a protective wall around the perimeter, part of which still stands today.

The town is generally acknowledged as being the cultural capital of Essex, with several museums and galleries. There are many shops with rare books, antiques and also a collection of Colchester-made clocks that are splendidly displayed in the 15th-century timber-framed Tymperleys Clock Museum.

## Colchester Castle

The work on Colchester Castle began in 1076 by William the Conqueror's steward, a man called Eudo. Eudo was one of William's most trusted followers and was rewarded with land and power. The design of the castle is believed to be the same as the White Tower at the Tower of London except that it was twice as large. It was built on the ruins of the Temple of Claudius and by using the temple vaults as its base, it became the largest castle ever built by the Normans. The keep stood about ninety feet high and was constructed of reused Roman stones and red bricks taken from the original building and others around the town.

In June of 1648, during the English Civil War, two Royalist commanders, Sir Charles Lucas and Sir George Lisle surrendered to General Fairfax of the Parliamentarian army after eleven weeks of fighting. Sir Lucas and Sir Lisle were executed in the grounds of the castle, a memorial to them can be seen in the gardens.

There is a fine museum in the castle with many interesting artifacts. The vaults can also be seen as part of a guided tour and is well worth a visit.
Open: 10:00 a.m. until 5:00 p.m. Monday through Saturday year round.
11:00 a.m. until 5:00 p.m. on Sundays from March to November.

## Colchester Zoo

The award-winning zoo is located on approximately sixty acres on the rolling hills of Essex. There are over two hundred animals from all over the world from the majestic African elephant to tiny monkeys. The zoo specializes in educational demonstrations of falconry and parrot displays.
Open: Daily from 9:30 a.m. until dusk.

*Colchester Castle*

Telephone: 01206 282939. Address: Maldon Road, Colchester.

**Bourne Mill**
Bourne Mill was once a 16th-century fishing lodge that was converted into a mill. Some of the machinery is still in good condition, and the beautiful millpond provides a great opportunity for wonderful photographs.
Open: 2:00 p.m. until 5:30 p.m. Sundays and Tuesdays only during June, July and August.

**The Oyster Festival**
As Britain's oldest recorded town, Colchester has a reputation for its ancient streets and houses. It is also famous for its oysters that are cultivated in the Colne River. The

custom of The Oyster Festival began in 1256 and is still enjoyed to this day. It begins on the last Friday of October with the Mayor of the town sailing downstream dredging the first oysters of the season. Besides the consumption of many oysters during the feast, The Queen's (or King's) health is toasted with a glass of gin accompanied by a slice of gingerbread. Many important people from the town and famous personalities celebrate the Oyster Festival each year. There are a few seats available for the public but these are in great demand. The high quality of the oysters from the area is well known, so a visit to the oyster fisheries is recommended.

## For more information:
Telephone: (0) 1206 282920. Address: Colchester Tourist Information Center. 1 Queen Street, Colchester. A walking tour of the town can be obtained through the Blue Badge Guide.

## Food for thought:
### Tilly's Tea Rooms
Tilly's Tea Rooms offers a great cup of coffee or a wonderful Cream Tea in the afternoon with homemade cakes and light sandwiches.
Telephone: (0)1206 560600. Address: 22 Trinity Street, Colchester.

## If you decide to stay:
### The George Hotel
The George Hotel was once a 16th-century coaching inn and still reflects the style and elegance of centuries past. Located in the heart of town, The George has a wonderful atmosphere with exposed wooden beams and inglenook fireplaces, which together make this a charming place to

stay. Meals are available all day including breakfast, lunch, afternoon Cream Tea and dinner.
Telephone: (0) 1206 578494. Address: 116 High Street, Colchester.

### The Rose & Crown Hotel
The hotel has recently been refurbished but has retained its character and appeal. Some bedrooms have gorgeous four-poster beds and beautiful exposed wooden beams. The hotel offers a full restaurant and extensive bar.
Telephone: (0)1206 866677. Address: Rose & Crown Hotel, East Gates, Colchester.

## How to get there:
There are Intercity services between Colchester and London Liverpool Street. For more information call National Rail Inquiry at (0) 8457 484950.

**By car**: Head northeast from London on the A12. You'll see signposts for Brentwood and Chelmsford. Be certain to bypass Chelmsford by staying on the A12 when it veers to the right just south of the city. Stay on the A12 all the way to Colchester. Follow signs to "City Centre". Colchester is about 60 miles away from central London, and the drive will take about 80 minutes.

# Greensted-juxta-Ongar

He was crowned King of East Anglia on Christmas Day in the year of 855, at the tender age of 15, and died when he was only 29 years old. King Edmund was a good and virtuous ruler who cared deeply for his people, but he perished at the hands of Ivar the Dane because he would not renounce his Christianity.

According to the Anglo-Saxon Chronicles (a detailed account of the history of England covering 1,000 years from Roman times to the middle of the 12th century) "...a great heathen force" of Vikings arrived in 865 on the eastern shores of England known as East Anglia. They lost no time in conquering every village in their path; ravaging and pillaging until nothing was left. Then came a threatening message to King Edmund from Ivar, the captain of the Danes, "You will surrender your possessions and your people to me or die." The king summoned his most faithful bishop for guidance but his suggestion that the king should flee was unacceptable. "...Alas bishop, I would rather die fighting so that my people might continue to possess their native land." The bishop informed the king that word had just come from the battlefields that his armies were defeated, all was lost and surrender or flee were the only options.

The Chronicles tell us King Edmund was captured, tortured unmercifully and suffered unmentionable terrors. The Dane offered Edmund his life if he would renounce Christ. He would not, and was lashed until he almost died. With every lash he cried Jesus' name, infuriating his captors. Finally, he was tied to a tree and killed by a hail of arrows so that "...hardly a place on his body was not covered with arrows..." He was then beheaded. As a final insult, the pirates hid King Edmund's head in the forest so that it could not be buried with his body.

Soon after King Edmund's death, the Britons and some reformed Danes began to regard him as a saint because of his courageous life and honorable death. A shrine was erected and pilgrims traveled from all over Britain to honor this great man.

It is thought the final resting-place for the remains of Saint Edmund is a town called Bury St. Edmunds, in Suffolk, but some believe his remains are in the churchyard at St. Andrews's church.

## What to see and do today:
### St. Andrews Church
The small, unique church of St. Andrews is believed to be the oldest wooden church in the world and is said to have held the remains of Saint Edmund for several days before their final destination to Bury Saint Edmunds centuries later. The location of the church, deep in the Essex countryside, is believed to have saved it from destruction by the Danes. The Chronicles say of the Danes, "...they made that which was very great such that it became nothing..."

Recent tests show that the church was not built during Saxon times as originally thought but was built around 1066. However, it is still considered to be the oldest wooden church in the world. The walls of the church are split oak trees, used vertically with the rounded, bark side facing the elements. These proved to be stout, sturdy walls that still remain to this day. During the 16th century, a flint chancel and little dormer windows were added, giving the church a pleasing and unusual appearance.

The church is quite dark inside, with shafts of light coming through the dormer windows. The nave has a wonderful carving of a wolf guarding a severed head. The legend of the wolf protecting the head began when friends of King Edmund found his body but not his head. As they searched the forest, they called their king's name and heard, "here, here, here." Eventually they found the head of their beloved king embraced in the paws of a large gray wolf. They believed the wolf was keeping guard until the king's men could reclaim it.

There is a strange alcove in the north wall of the church. This was possibly a Leper's Squint although not much of the altar can be seen from its location. Leper's Squints were usually angled in such a way that a person with leprosy or the plague could watch the priest administer the sermon and receive communion without actually making direct contact.

Alongside St. Andrew's church is a footpath called Essex Way. The path leads to Chipping Ongar, the next town. It is a pleasant walk through wheat fields and takes about half an hour. It is approximately one mile from Greensted.

## Neighboring places of interest:
### Chipping Ongar
Chipping Ongar is located about 2 miles east of Greensted by car. The name is thought to have derived from the Anglo-Saxon "Chipping," meaning market and grassland. During the 12th century permission was given for a weekly market in the village. It is believed to have taken place in the center of the village where the street is at its widest. It was later transferred to an area around The Old Market

House, a 16th-century building that still stands today together with two other buildings of the same period, The White House and Castle House.

**Waltham Abbey Church**
King Harold built the nave of the church around 1060. It is reputedly where he is buried after losing his life at the Battle of Hastings in 1066 against William the Conqueror. After the death of King Harold, his men collected his body from the battlefield and carried it to Waltham Abbey so he could be buried in the church he loved so much, but this cannot be substantiated.

The church was originally twice its current size. During the Reformation in 1540 the church was pulled down, leaving only the nave as a parish church. The church is in excellent condition and beautifully restored. The Crypt Center houses an exhibition of the history of the abbey and the town.
Open: Daily 10:00 a.m. until 6:00 p.m. 12:00 noon on Sunday and 11:00 a.m. on Wednesdays.
Telephone: (0) 1992 767897. Address: Highbridge Street, Waltham Abby.

**Royal Epping Forest**
Epping Forest is famous for being the hunting grounds for King Henry VII, King Henry VIII and his daughter, Elizabeth I. Hunting is now forbidden in the approximately 6,000 acres which sit astride the M11 to the west and north of Chipping Ongar. It is said that King Henry VIII was hunting in Epping Forest the day Ann Bolyn was beheaded and only returned to London when the gun salute at the Tower of London indicated the deed was done.

Essex folklore also tells us that Epping Forest was believed to be where Boadicea met her end, but once again this cannot be substantiated and is thought to be a romanticized version of the Iceni Queen's death.

Epping Forest was also a favorite place of Dick Turpin the highwayman. "Stand and deliver" was a frequent cry from this man who chose a highwayman's life rather than pursue an honorable trade. He was born on September 21, 1705, in the town of Hempstead. Much is made of Dick Turpin's exploits and the speed of Black Bess, his fabled horse, but he was no more than an everyday thief. After years of robbing travelers in Epping Forest, Turpin met his match when he called "stand and deliver" to Tom King, another highwayman. King roared with laughter and said, "Come brother Turpin, if you don't know me, I know you and would be glad of your company." The two men joined forces and began a reign of terror in the forest that lasted for years. In an attempt to confuse their pursuers, Turpin and King had their horses shoed with round horseshoes to confuse the Keepers of the Forest, a group of men whose duties were to keep law and order in the ancient forest.

Eventually a bounty of 200 pounds (sterling) was placed on Turpin's head, dead or alive. By a coincidence of bad luck and judgment, Turpin was apprehended after almost ten years of living outside the law. Turpin stood tall and arrogant when the judge passed the sentence, "Your country has found you guilty of a crime worthy of death, it is my office to pronounce sentence against you." His sentence, hanging, was carried out on Saturday April 7th, 1739. Records from the day tell us that he purchased a new coat and shoes for his hanging, in addition to hiring men and women to dress in fashionable coats and hats to escort him to the gallows. He reputedly bowed to the audience, which had gathered to watch the execution, and then, rather than die slowly by the hangman's noose, he threw himself out from the scaffold, dying instantly.

**North Weald Aerodrome**
The North Weald Aerodrome is home to several aviation clubs offering a variety of displays of veteran and classic aircraft from around the world. They include Spitfires, Yaks, Mustangs and Gnats. The most recent arrivals include an Estonian registered L29 Delfin and a Canadair-built T33 Silver Star in USAF Thunderbird's markings.

There are frequent "Fighter Meets" at the aerodrome, which is located approximately 3 miles from Greensted.
Open: By appointment from the Museum at Ad Astra House.
Telephone: (0) 1708 551780. Address: Ad Astra House, Hurricane Way, North Weald Airfield, North Weald, Essex.

## Food for thought:
### The Royal Oak Pub – Chipping Ongar
The Royal Oak Pub is a 15$^{th}$-century inn on the main road from London to East Anglia. Chipping Ongar was an important staging post for travelers making their way to Colchester and the East Coast. The pub was purchased by a local brewery in 2000 but still retains the wonderful atmosphere with a Folk Club meeting there every two weeks singing the Blues and Jazz. There is no restaurant on the premises but snack food is available.
Telephone: (0) 1277 363893. Address: 99 High Street, Chipping Ongar.

## If you decide to stay:
### The Packford Hotel
The Packford hotel is situated on the outskirts of Epping Forest in a quiet residential area only 30 minutes from central London. The decor in the hotel is traditional with a charming Victorian-style conservatory that leads to attractive gardens.

Telephone: (0) 20850 42642. Address: 16 Snakes Lane West, Woodford Green.

## For more information:
Telephone: (0) 1245 283400, Essex Tourist Information Center.

## How to get there:
There is direct train service from London to Epping on the Underground, Central Line. Travel time is about 50 minutes.

**By car**: Head out of London on the M11 motorway towards Cambridge. Exit the M11 at exit number 7 and turn left onto B1393 signposted for Epping. Continue on B1393 into Epping town center. To reach Greensted, take the B181 northeast out of Epping towards Tyler's Green. Turn right (east) onto the A414 at the B181/A414 junction roundabout. Take A414 to Chipping Ongar. At the roundabout, head south into the village. Just as you start to leave the village and before the junction with A113, turn right. Head west for about a mile to Greensted. Epping is about 22 miles away from central London, and the drive will take about 35 minutes.

# Castle Hedingham

William the Conqueror carefully chose the men who accompanied him on his invasion of England in 1066. The deVeres were fighting men and were pleased to have been given the opportunity to fight with their leader. They were richly rewarded for their loyalty with land and livestock that was originally owned by Ulwine, a Saxon Thane or baron. The family soon became one of the most influential in Essex and ruled there for the next 600 years.

In 1098, Aubrey deVere II took part in the first Crusade. According to legend, a strange event took place on the battlefield. A fierce fight raged between deVere and the Sultan of Persia for the city of Antioch. DeVere's troops were at a disadvantage because of the unknown terrain and also that dusk was falling. Suddenly, a light shone on the standard of deVere casting a brilliant light consisting of a five-pointed star that illuminated the field of battle. Believing this to be a good omen, deVere's troops continued the battle under the light of the star and were victorious. The five-pointed star or "molette" was added to the coat of arms of the deVere family and is one of the most recognized in medieval heraldry today.

Robert deVere inherited the estate from his brother Aubrey deVere, who was known as one of King John's "evil councilors." It was rumored that Aubrey had a close and unusual relationship with the King and greatly influenced him. When Robert inherited the estate, his political aspirations were very different from that of his brother. King John's cruel and unfair treatment of his barons and subjects had caused civil unrest in the country and Robert believed he had found a solution to this unhappiness.

In an attempt to bring law and order to the country, Robert deVere collaborated with 24 other barons to design and draft a document called the Magna Carta. The document clearly stated the rights of inheritance by widows, the rights of barons over their estates and that no man was above the law, even the reigning monarch. In essence… "No freeman shall be taken, imprisoned…or in any other way destroyed…except by the lawful judgment of his peers, or by the law of the land. To no one will we deny or delay right or justice."

King John signed the Magna Carta at Runnymede in 1215. The Magna Carta changed the course of history in England, providing law and justice over a strife-ridden country.

## What to see and do today:
### Hedingham Castle
The castle was built between 1130 and 1152 on land that originally belonged to a Saxon. The keep is all that is left of the original castle but this alone is impressive, standing 110 feet high with 12-foot-deep walls at the base. It is one of the finest keeps in the country. Although not as pleasing to the eye as other castles and keeps, we can see it was built with defense in mind. The austere and seemingly impregnable walls must have seemed a daunting task for an invading army. King John laid siege to the castle in 1215, causing terrible damage. He was victorious but it was short-lived; he died in 1216 and Robert deVere was reinstated in his magnificent home.

The stones used for the castle were ashlar blocks brought from quarries in Cambridgeshire, which is about 30 miles from Hedingham. The task of hauling such a quantity of stone would have cost a fortune, but the deVeres considered themselves worthy of the finest castle that could be built. The area around the castle would not have been very different from today. The castle grounds would have been cleared of trees so potential attacks could easily be seen by the archers on the towers, giving a clear line of fire. Boiling oil poured from the ramparts and stones would have been used as a defense.

The Norman influence is evident in the keep. The Norman masons were fine craftsmen and their expertise is legendary. The spectacular arch in the banqueting hall is believed to be the largest Norman arch in England. A minstrel gallery runs atop the amoury walls and provides a wonderful view of the hall below.

Hedingham Castle was a favorite with the reigning monarch. Over the years, King Henry VII, King Henry VIII, and his daughter Elizabeth I spent time with the deVeres in this superb home in the heart of Essex.

There is a splendid example of a Tudor Bridge spanning the dry moat that leads to the Inner Bailey. There is also an 18th-century dovecote nestled in the exquisite gardens.

There are many attractions each year at the castle, including jousting tournaments, medieval and craft festivals, medieval sieges and an Elizabethan Yuletide celebration. Open: 10:00 a.m. until 5:00 p.m., from one week before Easter through the end of October.
Telephone: (0) 1787 460261. Address: Bayley Street, Castle Hedingham.

## The Village
Castle Hedingham is a pretty village laid out in a triangular fashion with cottages ringing the church. During the reign of King Henry VII, John deVere was given important positions at the court and it's believed he used this power to give special privileges to the village. A charter to hold a market on Mondays was granted, which brought tradesmen and travelers to the village bringing wealth to the community.

Opposite the entrance to Hedingham Castle grounds is a row of delightful cottages on Castle Lane. The cottages are painted pink, green and yellow, and show excellent examples of thatching with intricate designs. The pink and green cottages have the traditional "eyebrow" dormer windows and are decorated with a wooden, lattice-style design.

## St. Nicholas Church
St. Nicholas is a magnificent church built under the direction of the deVere family. The body of the church is older than the 1616 brick tower and includes an unusual Norman wheel window. Its pointed gothic arches are typical of what is called the Transitional style of church architecture.

## Colne Valley Railway
The pretty, award-winning station is the beginning of a pleasant ride on a section of railway originally known as the Colne Valley line. This steam railway uses the largest collection of operational heritage railway engines, carriages and wagons in the country. Special events throughout the year include a murder mystery evening and Thomas the Tank Engine days. Call for more information. Telephone: (0) 1787 461174. Address: Yeldham Road, Castle Hedingham.

## Food for thought:
### The Old Moot House
The Old Moot House restaurant serves lunch and dinner in a 15th-century half-timbered building once used as the village meetinghouse. Some parts of the building date from between 1320 and 1370. A varied à la Carte menu including vegetarian meals is available.
Telephone: (0)1787 460342. Address: 1st James Street, Castle Hedingham.

## If you decide to stay:
### Rosemary Farm
Rosemary Farm consists of two small cottages in a barn conversion offering a lounge, kitchen, one double room and one single bedroom. A shower, toilet, patio and parking area are all conveniently situated. There are great countryside walks to the village, pubs and restaurant.
Tel (0) 1787461653/370399. Address: Rosemary Lane, Castle Hedingham.

## Neighboring places of interest:

Finchingfield is a beautiful village said to be the most photographed in Essex. The homes around St. Nicholas, the parish church, have a wealth of pargeting (raised plasterwork) on the exterior and beautifully kept gardens. The Village Green and pond appear idyllic with mallard ducks, Canada geese and moor hens. This area in particular is the most photographed in the village. The Green is surrounded with wonderful tea rooms, pubs, antique and specialty shops.

### Finchingfield Windmill
The windmill is a small 18th-century post mill. Recently renovated, it has one pair of stones and tail pole winding.

Open: On the third Sunday of each month from 2:00 p.m. until 5:00 p.m.
Telephone: (0) 1621 828162. Address: Havering Road, Finchingfield.

**The Almshouses**
Built in the early 17th century, the attractive row of Almshouses line the road towards the Village Green. They are painted the traditional white with black exposed wooden beams supporting the overhanging upper story. They were originally built for retired clergy and other needy people of the town and are still supported by the church of St. Nicholas. They are not open to the public.

**St. John the Baptist**
The church of St. John the Baptist was probably built around the 12th century, with the majority of the work completed in the 14th century. Historical records from 1735 tell us that a beautiful spire "…lofty and leaded and was blown down at Cromwell's exit." The Rood Screens are a testament to the excellent workmanship of medieval woodcarvers. They were created in the 15th century and considered to be the finest screens in Essex. The blue enameled clock is said to keep excellent time, even with Big Ben in London.

**Spains Hall**
Spains Hall sits back from the road in its entire splendor but it's rumored to have a sad and unhappy episode to its history. William Kempe and his wife lived at the hall during the period between 1555 and 1628. He was an unhappy man, full of insecurities and jealous of his beautiful wife. One day in 1621 in a fit of rage, he accused her of being unfaithful to him, hurting her deeply. When he realized the accusations were unjustified, he promised her he would never speak again. He also dug the first of many

fishponds as a pleasing gesture to his wife. Although his loving and faithful wife died two years later, the guilt never ceased and he continued to torment himself.

As the years passed, Kempe continued his self-imposed penance of silence and excavated a fishpond every year in his wife's memory. Finally, in 1628, his health deteriorated drastically and although he tried to call for help, he could not make a sound. He was mortified and the very shock of being unable to speak caused his death.

Only two of the seven fishponds can be seen today although even those have merged into one. However, a good sleuth can detect the other five by the topography of the gardens.
Open: The house is not open to the public, but the gardens are available to visitors by arrangement.
Telephone:  (0) 1371 810598 for a tour around Spains Hall and other places of interest in the village.

## Food for thought:
### The Causeway Tea Rooms
The Causeway Tea Rooms delivers an excellent view of the Village Green and a perfect place for morning coffee, a light lunch or a Cream Tea in the afternoon.

## If you decide to stay:
### The Red Lion Inn
The Red Lion is a 16th-century inn with four guest rooms available. The bedrooms are decorated with a traditional flair and have wonderful exposed wooden beams. The inn has an à la Carte menu as well as the usual pub food. It is located across the road almshouses leading to the Village Green.

Telephone: (0) 1371 810400. Address: Church Hill, Finchingfield.

## How to get there:

There is no direct train service from London to Hedingham, so the easiest way to get to there is by car.

**By car**: Head out of London on the M11 motorway towards Cambridge. Continue north to the A120 exit (number 8). Take the A120 towards Great Dunmow. At Great Dunmow take the B1057 north to Finchingfield. To reach Hedingham from Finchingfield, leave the village towards the east on B1053 to Wethersfield. In the village of Wethersfield turn left towards Sible Hedingham. Continue for about 5 miles. Continue through Sible Hedingham and to the junction with A1017. Turn left and then right almost immediately on to B1058 into Castle Hedingham. Hedingham is about 50 miles away from central London, and the drive will take about 70 minutes.

# Saffron Walden

From the Great Plague of 1348 came the grim nursery rhyme, *Ring a Ring of Roses, a Pocketful of Posies*. The nursery rhyme suggested the deadly progress of the disease as it ravaged its victims' bodies. Unsure of how the plague was spreading, a person would wear saffron in a posy around the neck or hold a nosegay to their nose in an attempt to ward off the disease.

Originally saffron was cultivated for use as a yellow/orange dye for the wool trade and also for culinary purposes, but the height of the saffron trade was during the 17th century when it was considered an affective deterrent against the plague.

Five hundred years ago, the fields of Saffron Walden were awash with the purple hue of the saffron crocus in flower. The flowers were harvested in October, before the petals were completely opened. The orange stigmas, the only part of the flower used, were separated and dried on racks over slow fires. Twenty to thirty thousand flowers would generate approximately one pound of saffron that would be crushed and pounded into cakes. The purple petals covered the ground like massive blankets, but the villagers knew their cultivation of saffron would provide wealth and security for their families and future generations.

Folklore tells us that in the 14th century, a pilgrim smuggled the first saffron corm (a tuber-like stem) from its Middle Eastern origin into England in the hollow of his staff. The lush arable land of Essex, known for the cultivation of barley and corn was now host to a new and more lucrative market that could be tithed by the church. The clergy of Walden had the legitimate claim to place a tax on all saffron grown outside the Abbey boundaries.

The wealth of the village grew at a remarkable rate. The Parish Church of St. Mary the Virgin was built, and beautiful, half-timbered homes sprung up often with splendid pargeting (exterior raised plasterwork) from the local craftsman.

## What to see and do today:

Saffron Walden is a market town, full of hustle and bustle. The exteriors of the homes are often finished in stucco style and are painted in pastels of pink, green, yellow and blue. Some are painted a stark white with the exterior beams in a shiny, black, paint finish. Sometimes the upper levels of these homes overhang in such a fashion that it seems as though they will topple into the street at any moment.

The 14th-century building on Castle Street, known as the Sun Inn, is decorated with 17th-century pargeting and depicts a local hero, Tom Hickathrift, fighting an Ogre. Folklore tells us that the monster ogre was hatched from a cock's egg and could kill a person merely by looking at them. Tom Hickathrift, a traveling knight, slew the ogre by wearing special armor that reflected the ogre's eyes back on himself. Topsell, a 17th-century historian wrote, "their owne shapes were reflected upon their owne faces, and so they dyed." The saffron crocus is also depicted on the walls of the Sun Inn as a testament to the lucrative influence of the flower in the history of the town.

*Oliver Cromwell's Headquarters 1647*
*– Now the Old Sun Inn*

**Audley End**
Audley End House is a magnificent country home built by the Earl of Suffolk in 1603–14. He built this splendid house because he wanted to impress James I by offering him luxury accommodation in the countryside. However, the earl fell out of favor with the King and the house was altered and reduced in size by two-thirds, (although even at its present size, it is spectacular). The architectural talent of this beautiful home together with the contents of silverware, paintings, a natural history collection and a stained-glass window depicting the Last Supper, make it well worth a visit.
Open: 11:00 a.m. until 6:00 p.m. April 1 through September 30, Wednesday through Sunday. Winter hours: 10:00 a.m. until 3:00 p.m. October 1 through November 1, Wednesday through Sunday.

Telephone: (0) 1799 522399. Address: West of Saffron Walden on B1383.

**St. Mary the Virgin**
It is believed that a church has been on the site of St. Mary the Virgin since the 13th century; however, the aisles and nave were rebuilt in the 15th century taking approximately one hundred years to complete. The saffron crocus flower can be seen on the Communion Rail and in the north window where a set of crocuses is designed as a scallop.

**The Sun Inn**
The Sun Inn, once the headquarters of parliamentarian Oliver Cromwell, now holds wonderful antiques and an extensive book collection to browse through. The exterior walls are decorated with extraordinary pargeting depicting the saffron crocus. There is also a notation over the door recording the fact that Cromwell used this inn as his headquarters during the English Civil War.

**Bridge End Gardens**
The beautiful Victorian gardens at Bridge End with their delicately manicured topiary, rose garden, lead fountain and statues are a wonderful place to enjoy. The maze is a scaled-down version of the famous maze at Hampton Court (London). The gardens are a result of the Gibson's, a local influential family of Quakers. It was Atkinson Gibson who first conceived the idea and partly laid out the plans for the gardens in 1794. On his death, his son, Francis Gibson, continued the work. The beautiful views from the pavilions, the balustrade walls and the Dutch garden are a testament to the love of two philanthropists who spent their wealth providing this exquisite garden for the residents of the town and its visitors.

Open: To the public at all times. The maze is open daily but gated 10:00 a.m. until 5:00 p.m.

### The Maze
There are two mazes at Saffron Walden, the first in Bridge End Gardens. The second is called the Turf Maze and lies on The Castle Green, also known as The Common. The age of the maze is unknown although records show it was reconstructed in 1699 for about fifteen shillings. Legend has it that mazes were created for people who behaved badly and needed to reflect on their conduct. They would be placed in the center of the maze and instructed to find their way out. The difficulties they encountered trying to escape the concentric design were supposed to help them understand the choices given to them in life and therefore to consider any decision they made thereafter very carefully.

### The Museum
The museum has an award-winning collection of ancient artifacts including; Ages of Man, nature of woodland animals, ceramics, glass and costumes from the ages. The museum is also the resting place of the human skin found at St. Botolph's Church, Hadstock. It is reputed to be that of a Danish pirate who committed heresy, was flayed, and his skin nailed to the door of the church.
Open: 10:00 a.m. until 5 p.m. Monday through Saturday, March to October. Sundays 2:00 p.m. until 5 p.m.
Open: 2:00 p.m. until 4:30 p.m. November through February.
Telephone: (0) 1799 510444. Address: Located close to the maze on the Common.

## Food for thought:
**The Queen's Head Inn** is a 14th-century inn known for serving a fine selection of fish each day, depending on the

catch of the day. They also serve casseroles, and great desserts too.
Telephone: (0) 1799 522251. Address: Littlebury, close to Saffron Walden.

## If you decide to stay:
**North Hall Farm Guest House** is a 17th-century farm home. The rooms have bathrooms en suite with televisions and coffee/tea appliances. Car rental is available at competitive rates. There is also a service to and from the airport and railway stations.
Telephone: (0) 1799 543429. Address: North Hall Farm, North Hall Road, Quendon, Saffron Walden.

## For more information:
Saffron Walden Tourist Information Center: (0) 1799 510444.

## Neighboring places of interest:
The small village of **Hadstock** is approximately seven miles north of Saffron Walden. St. Botolph's, a Saxon church, boasts of having the oldest door in regular use in Britain as mentioned in the Guinness Book of Records. The legend revolves around St. Botolph, who began a small monastery at Icanho in the kingdom of East Anglia. It is believed he is buried somewhere in the church grounds. In 1144 the Monks of Ely referred to Hadstock as "that place sanctified to religion in days of old by the Holy Botolph, there at rest."

There was also another legend, but this myth proved to be true. The main door of the church dated approximately 1020 was once said to have had the skin of a Dane nailed to the door. It is reputed that a Dane was flayed alive for committing sacrilege and his skin was nailed to the door as an example of punishment to others considering heresy. When the door was removed for repairs recently, skin was discovered under the hinges. It was sent for analysis, which determined it was human and, most likely, the skin of the Dane mentioned in the legend. It is now in the museum at Saffron Walden.

In St. Botolph's churchyard, there is an unusual headstone to Michael Ayrton who was known as a master maze builder. It holds an 18" double spiral bronze labyrinth replica of the Arkville labyrinth Ayrton in New York. The tombstone is located at the northeast corner of the churchyard on left-hand side of the gravel path. Visitors to Ayrton's graveside have run their fingers through the bronze plaque trying to locate the beginning and end of the puzzle. Even in death, Ayrton still has the ability to perplex people.

## How to get there:
There is train service from London to Wendens Ambo, which is about three miles from Saffron Walden. As there is no train or bus service directly to Saffron Walden from London, the easiest way to get there is by car.

**By car**: Head north from London on the M11. You'll see signposts for Stansted Airport and Cambridge. Stay on the M11 for about twenty-five miles. Take the A120 exit towards Bishop's Stortford. At the first roundabout, take the A120. Go through the next roundabout, and at the next roundabout, take the B1383 towards the north. Stay on the B1383 to just south of Wendens Ambo, then take the B1052 to Saffron Walden. Saffron Walden is approximately 50 miles away from central London.

# Thaxted

Gustav Holst, composer, fell in love with Thaxted on first sight when he arrived in the winter of 1913. He and his wife Isobel stayed at the Enterprise, a small guest house in Town Street for a five-day walking holiday. They enjoyed their visit, the people and the town so much that he was determined to return. The following year, Holst leased a small house called Monk Street Cottage, and he and Isobel settled in to make Thaxted their home.

It was a difficult time in England. World War I had just started and anyone with a name such as von Holst (which was his full surname) was looked upon with skepticism and distrust. Holst was eyed with suspicion, especially as he was seen walking alone for hours each day. This came to the attention of the local police constabulary, who felt obliged to keep a watch on the strange man as he walked around the village. A policeman's report noted, "Many rumors are current about this man, but nothing can be traced against him."

Slowly Holst began to make friends but there was one person in particular, Conrad Noel, who became a close friend. Conrad was deeply involved with village life and introduced Holst to members of Saint John the Baptist Church and the choir. Soon Holst was known warmly as "our Mr. Von" and in 1916 he organized, conducted and played the organ at the Whitsun Festival. One weekend, he brought students from London to join with the Thaxted choir in an unforgettable time of singing and rejoicing. A member of the congregation was quoted as saying that Holst could make the organ "speak." The organ Holst used to compose some of his famous works is still in Saint John the Baptist Church.

Here in this peaceful town of Thaxted, Holst was able to work on his *Planets Suite* as well as many of his other symphonies. In 1924, while recovering from a bout of illness, he completed *Choral Symphony* and wrote to a friend, "It has been wonderful to sit all day in the garden and watch the symphony grow up alongside of the flowers and vegetables, and then to find that it is done!"

The ancient town of Thaxted has changed little from maps of the 14th century. As with most villages and towns of that period, the houses and buildings were built around the parish church and other important buildings in the township.

In the late 1300s, there were so many cutlers (makers of cutlery) in the town that they decided to organize a guild and build a Guildhall as a meeting place. They selected a site opposite Hall Gate, entrance to the Manor of Thaxted.

It's believed that the manor and the surrounding buildings were destroyed during the Peasants' Revolt of 1381, but the Guildhall still stands to this day. The cutlers also built the spectacular church and dedicated it to St. Lawrence, the Patron Saint of Cutlers. The Guildhall and the church are the oldest buildings in town and are as impressive today as they were almost 600 years ago. The town's official crest shows crossed swords as a tribute to the cutlery trade and the prosperity they brought to the town of Thaxted.

## What to see and do today:

"There is no town in north Essex — and very few in England — to equal in beauty, compactness, and juxtaposition of medieval and Georgian architecture as the town of Thaxted." — Sir John Betjeman.

### The Church of St. John the Baptist, St. Mary and St. Lawrence

The church is quite exquisite and still dominates the town. It has been described as one of the most beautiful and architecturally pleasing in the country. The foundations were laid and work began on the church in 1340, and it was completed in 1510. No one knows for sure who the original benefactors of the church were but the Cutlers, townspeople and the House of Clare who owned the Manor were all thought to be instrumental in its construction. The influential family of the House of Clare had connections to the Crown, so it is assumed that royalty also contributed to the initial funds.

The walls of St. John the Baptist Church are made of flint with decorations in limestone. The roofs are constructed of lead, with the exception of the tiled north and south porch chambers. During construction of the church the artisans were asked to carve their own likeness in the rafters. Some have portrayed themselves with smiling faces, others are quite grim, but yet some have shown a sense of humor by poking their tongues out. There are various ancient chests around the church holding age-old linens that are still used during services. The splendid organ used by Holst as he composed *The Planets Suite* and some of his other works sits quietly against a wall in the church.

It is believed the famous St. Thomas à Beckett, who was killed at Canterbury Cathedral on supposed orders of King Henry II, was interred under the floor of the church.

**The Guild Hall**
During the 14th century, Thaxted was a thriving, town growing with the cutlery trade. In 1381, the Poll Tax returns show 249 male tradesmen. Of these, 78 were cutlers while other men were associated with the cutlery trade. As there was no iron ore in Essex, it was shipped from Kent, therefore providing jobs in that county. Other raw products such as charcoal and wood for the fires were also in great demand, supplying jobs for a country ravaged by the plague in which approximately only a third of the population survived.

Construction of the Guildhall probably began around 1393 by the cutlers, who needed a place to meet. The scale and design of the building has changed little over almost 600 years, and offers a rare insight into the minds of these extraordinary men. The building has been used not only as a guild but also as a school and administrative offices.
Open: Sundays only from 2:00 p.m. until 6:00 p.m., Easter to September.

**Almshouses**
Almshouses can be found in many towns and villages around the country. After the Reformation by King Henry VIII, some income from the churches was used to build almshouses for retired clergy, knights and other needy people of high status. They offer the bare minimum of hospitality and usually comprise of one bedroom, a small sitting room and kitchen. Many almshouses today have been converted to quaint cottages often with thatched roofs and exterior gingerbread (decorative wooden designs).

There are two almshouses in Thaxted, alongside the church with the windmill in the background. One is painted dark pink with a wonderful thatch and the other is painted a pale salmon color with lead windows and white gingerbread. When they were first built, they were divided into separate dwellings probably housing about 16 people. Nowadays, they have each been converted into one long home.

**Thaxted Windmill**
John Webb built the windmill in 1804 on the site of an earlier windmill, which was demolished in 1770. Webb was a local farmer who also owned a tile and brick company, so we can assume that during its construction much of the materials came from his own firm. It was in use for approximately 100 years and then fell into disrepair. The Thaxted Windmill Trust was established in the 1970's to restore the windmill.
Open: 2:00 p.m. until 6:00 p.m. Saturday and Sunday from May through September.

## Food for thought:
**The Cake Table Tea Room**
Scrumptious homemade cakes, morning coffee, light lunches and Cream Teas in the afternoon are the Cake Table's specialties. The Cake Table won the award for the Top Tea Place in 1991.
Telephone: (0) 1371 831206. Address: 4/5 Fishmarket Street, Thaxted.

## A place to stay:
**Crossways Guest House**
Crossways Guest House is located across the road from the famous Guildhall. It is a $16^{th}$-century building with bathrooms en suite. There are only two bedrooms in this small guest house but every effort is made to make guests welcome and comfortable.

Telephone: (0) 1371 830348. Address: 32 Town Street, Thaxted.

**The Swan Hotel**
The Swan offers 21 fully-equipped bedrooms with bathrooms en suite. There is a large function room and a well-catered restaurant with a varied menu. Bar meals are available on request.
Telephone: (0) 1371 830321. Address: The Bull Ring, Thaxted.

## Neighboring places of interest:
### Little Dunmow
Little Dunmow lies about eight miles south of Thaxted. It is an ancient village rich in history. Domesday Book records of 1086 show Ralph Baynard as Lord of Little Dunmow. In 1104, either Baynard's wife or sister built a priory and started a custom that is still in effect today: giving a flitch (side) of bacon to any couple who can swear to marital harmony for twelve months and a day.

The custom began with the idea of promoting marital harmony to a couple by offering them a prize and jubilant praise from the village folk. To qualify for the prize, the couple had to swear by means of reciting a rhyme while kneeling on two pointed stones in the churchyard. If the couple could convince the congregation of their commitment to each other, they were awarded the flitch of bacon and carried through the village seated on a chair.

The following Ancient Rhyme describes the ceremony:
*You shall swear by custom and confession,*
*That you ne'er made nuptial transgression,*
*Nor since you were married man and wife,*
*By household brawls, or contentious strife*
*Or otherwise, at bed or board,*

*Offend each other in deed or word:*
*Or, since the Parish Clerk said, Amen,*
*Wished yourselves unmarried again;*
*Or in a twelvemonth and a day,*
*Repented, even in thought, any way;*
*But continued true, in thought and desire,*
*As when you joined hands in holy quire.*
*If to these conditions, without any fear,*
*Of your own accord, you freely swear,*
*A whole flitch of bacon you shall receive,*
*And bear it hence with love and good leave:*
*For this is our custom at Dunmow well known,*
*Tho' the pleasure be ours, the bacon's your own.*

The church in Little Dunmow is quite small and narrow. It was formed from the south aisle and several arches from the nave of the original priory church. There is a chair in the church, which is said to have carried the winners of the Flitch of Bacon, although this has yet to be validated.

## How to get there:
There is no bus or rail service to Thaxted.

**By car:** Take the M11 motorway northeast out of London towards Cambridge. Travel on the M11 to Exit 8, A120 signpost for Stanstead Airport, and go left. Go through the first roundabout, staying on A120. At the second roundabout, take the B1383 to the north. Stay on B1383 for just over one mile and then take B1051 on the right to Thaxted. Thaxted is about 46 miles from central London.

# *Kent*

## Cobham

"Remember, remember the 5th of November, gunpowder, treason and plot." This ancient rhyme is still sung by English children today as they prepare an effigy of Guy Fawkes and place him atop a bonfire. An heir of the de Cobham family was tried for treason because of his supposed involvement in the Gunpowder Plot of 1605 — an unsuccessful attempt to blow up the Houses of Parliament and destroy the monarchy.

The village and much of the surrounding countryside were home to the de Cobham family, who dominated the village for nearly 400 years. The name of Cobham is considered to be of Anglo-Saxon origin and possibly derived from a personal name such as Cobba. During the period from 1360–70, the village grew in size under the direction of Sir John de Cobham, who rebuilt the parish church of St. Mary and built the College that stands in the rear of the church.

Robert Cecil was born on June 1, 1563, with a slight hump on his back. He was the only surviving child of William Cecil and Mildred, daughter of Sir Anthony Cooke. He married into the family of de Cobham in 1589 when he took Elizabeth Brooke, daughter of William Brooke, Lord Cobham, as his bride.

Cecil's father, Lord Burghley, was a career politician rising to the positions of Secretary of State in 1558–72 and then Lord Treasurer 1572–98. He was a resolute puritan and the most trusted advisor to Queen Elizabeth I. He worked closely with Sir Francis Walsingham to devise a complex network of spies and double agents that helped uncover a plot by English Catholics to overthrow the Queen. It was known as the Babington Plot of 1586 and involved a carefully orchestrated group of men, working in the interests of the Catholic Mary Queen of Scotland, to kill Queen Elizabeth. The intrigue, forged documents and denial of Queen Mary of any complicity did not save her from execution; she was beheaded on February 8, 1587, at Fotheringhay.

Lord Burghley had aspirations that his son Cecil would follow in his footsteps, and provided private tutors early in his son's development to further that wish. Young Cecil was tutored at home and later attended Cambridge and traveled extensively abroad, mostly in France.

By all accounts, Cecil did follow in his father's footsteps and accomplished more in his life than his father expected. He proved to be a skilled and influential politician, rising through the ranks to become a member of the Privy Council at the tender age of 28, the youngest member ever. In 1589, Cecil married Elizabeth Brooke, daughter to William Cooke, Lord Cobham. They had two children together; first a daughter, Frances and then a son, William.

As Cecil's career developed, there were many clashes of opinions in the Elizabethan court, mostly with Devereux, the Earl of Essex. They both coveted the position of Master of the Court of Wards but Cecil successfully maneuvered Devereux into a hopeless situation with Ireland, which effectively finished his political career, paving the way for Cecil's victory.

When Queen Elizabeth died in 1603, King James I came to power. Cecil had carefully structured a good relationship with the king in anticipation of Elizabeth's death and the King rewarded him with several titles, such as Baron Cecil of Essindene, Viscount Cranborne and, finally, the Earldom of Salisbury.

The Gunpowder Plot of November 5, 1605 to blow up the Houses of Parliament and destroy King James I was thought by some to be a wicked scheme organized by Jesuit priests in retaliation for the government's anti-Catholic ruling. To this day, there are suspicions about Robert Cecil's part in the plan. Some believe it was a plot instigated by Cecil himself to gain appreciation from the king and further secure his political ambitions. In all, thirteen men were accused of treason after torture and a written confession by Guy Fawkes, who was caught red-handed in the cellars of Westminster trying to ignite barrels of gunpowder. The close relationship with William Parker, Lord Monteagle, who was later identified as a prime conspirator in the plot, did not help the clouds of suspicion hanging over Cecil. Cecil's brother-in-law, Lord Cobham, as well as Cobham's younger brother George Brooke, was implicated in the conspiracy. Cecil and Lord Cobham escaped execution but George did not.

After the Gunpowder Plot, the death of Elizabeth and several political disasters, Cecil's physical condition deteriorated. There were harsh rumors about his health problems being caused by the pox rather than an advanced state of scurvy, as some believed. It is said that he had weeping sores that must have been excruciatingly painful. In the spring of 1612, he traveled to Bath in an attempt to relieve his suffering in the healing waters of the spa. He died on May 24, 1612, and left substantial debts totaling over 30,000 pounds sterling; much of his estate was sold to repay this debt. After his death, political satire of the day suggested that a "crooked back meant a crooked man" but even during Cecil's lifetime he was the cause of derisive comments by Queen Elizabeth and King James who often called him "the little elf."

The 5th of November is still celebrated in England with fireworks and bonfires, upon which an effigy of Guy Fawkes is placed to commemorate the foiled plot.

## What to see and do today:

The village is quite small with ancient houses surrounding St. Mary's church. There are many interesting buildings, from a flint home built in the early 14th century that was probably used by the clergy, as well as many brick-and-weather-board cottages.

There is some evidence of "fire marks" in the village. This legacy began after the Great Fire of London in 1666 when parishes were made responsible for providing county fire brigades. For a fee, insurance companies offered their own protection in the form of a band of burly men decked out in splendid uniforms. The men would arrive at a house in flames, only to let the house burn to the ground because it didn't have the necessary fire mark of their company. Competition between the companies was high and the men often clashed physically, to the detriment of the burning building. Fire marks were usually placed above the door and were easily recognizable. They were originally made of lead with a specific number, indicating the particular insurance company.

**Cobham Hall**
The magnificent ancestral home of the de Cobham family is now used as girls' school. It was built in the 16th century of red brick with accents of stone in the archways imported from Caen. During the next two hundred years, additions in the form of extra stories, covered corridors and courtyards further enhanced the original building.

The de Cobhams, either in the hall itself or maintaining the grounds and kitchen gardens, employed most of the people in the village. The original estate was comprised of approximately 1,800 acres and included farmlands and forests.
Open: April, July and August. Wednesday, Thursday and Sunday from 2:00 p.m. until 5:00 p.m. All tours are guided and subject to change. Call for more information. Telephone: (0) 1474 823371/824319. Address: Cobham Village.

**St. Mary's Church**
As with most parish churches, St. Mary sits on the highest ground of the village. The chancel is what remains of an earlier church built in 1220. The de Cobhams appear to have regarded the church as their personal chapel since their place of burial is particularly large even for a "wool" church, as they were (and are still) known today. An intense period of building began in 1360–70 and is recognized as such on a brass in the church stating Sir John de Cobham as "the Founder of this Place." He is also responsible for building the splendid college in the rear of the church.

There are magnificent brasses in the church that can be rubbed by appointment. In the chancel, there is an extraordinary table tomb dedicated to the Brooke family. The effigies of Lord Cobham and his wife are in a honey-colored alabaster, which is beautifully detailed by master craftsmen. On the base of the tomb there are tiny figurines depicting the couples' 10 sons and 4 daughters kneeling in prayer.

The rare Tilting Helmets seen in the chancel are copies of the originals currently in the Tower of London. There are three jousting helmets and one armet with a Saracen's head funerary crest. In medieval times, the helmet of the deceased was carried before the funeral procession. After the burial, it was placed in the church as a sign of respect and honor.

**Painshill Park**
Painshill Park is considered one of Europe's finest gardens. The creator, The Honorable Charles Hamilton, took the remains of an abbey and transformed it into a paradise of beautiful gardens that include a Gothic temple and a grotto. Hamilton was a gifted painter and designer, and his influence can be seen throughout the ornamental landscape. There is also a Chinese bridge over a 14-acre serpentine lake that uses a waterwheel to bring fresh water from the river.

More than 60 species of birds have been seen in the park and a variety of small mammals make it their home. An ancient and rare breed of sheep called the Jacob graze in the park; they are distinctive with their black-and-white markings.
Telephone: (0) 1932 868113. Address: Portsmouth Road, Cobham.

# Food for thought:
## Ye Olde Leather Bottle Hotel
Ye Olde Leather Bottle has a special menu each day that is listed on a chalkboard, but also serves traditional pub food such as sausage and mash, fish and chips, steaks

and curries. Vegetarian meals are served on request. There is a fine selection of beer and ales served in the lounge bar where a roaring fire will great you on a cold winter's day.

In the summer the beer garden offers a delightful place to rest and enjoy a pint of the local brew.

Telephone: (0) 1474 814327. Address: 54-56 The Street, Cobham.

## A place to stay:
### Ye Olde Leather Bottle Hotel

The inn was built in 1629 and was a royalist meeting place during the reign of Charles I. In 1720, a leather bottle containing gold sovereigns was found on the premises giving the inn its name. Charles Dickens was known to frequent the inn and used it in his novel, *Pickwick Papers*. In the story, Mr. Tracy Tupman drowned his sorrows in Ye Old Leather Bottle after being spurned by his sweetheart Rachel Wardle.

The inn has retained its charm over the centuries, and it known for its Dickensian associations and artifacts including original paintings, etchings and other memorabilia that surround the walls.

The inn has six guest bedrooms with exposed oak wooden beams, four-poster beds and en suite bathrooms (except the twin bedroom). The rooms are tastefully decorated in the Dickensian theme and provide an interesting and friendly atmosphere for the visitor.

Telephone: (0) 1474 814327. Address: 54-56 The Street, Cobham.

## Neighboring place of interest:
### Owletts Farmhouse
On the west outskirts of the village is the Owletts Farmhouse, owned by the National Trust. It was built in 1684 and is an excellent example of a 17th-century Kentish farmhouse, except for its unusual staircase and beautifully plastered ceiling. It is an unexpected pleasure to see craftsmen displaying their exquisite skill in the form of flowers, leaves and wreathes.

Open: April to September on Wednesday and Thursday only from 2:00 p.m. until 5:00 p.m.

Telephone: (0) 1892 890651. Address: The Street, Cobham.

## How to get there:
There is no direct train service from London to Cobham; however, it is possible to take a train from London Victoria to Sole Street from where Cobham can be reached by taxi. As there is no direct train or bus service to Cobham from London, the easiest way to get there is by car.

**By car**: Head southeast from London on A2 east out of London towards Rochester. About 3 miles before the junction with M2, look for Valley Drive and exit left. Go only a few hundred yards and turn left on Hever Court Road. Again after a short distance turn left onto Henhurst Road. Travel south on Henhurst to Jenkyns Road, which leads straight into Cobham. Cobham is approximately 26 miles away from central London.

# Royal Tunbridge Wells

Henrietta Maria was only 15 years old when she arrived from France to marry Charles I, King of England. As she kneeled before him, it was said she uttered the words, "Sir, I have come to this country for your Majesty to use and command." A cold and distant relationship followed for several years but they eventually learned to love each other and produced 9 children. Their love endured, despite opposition in court, until Charles was tried for treason and lost his head at the Palace of Whitehall, London.

King Charles, at 25 years of age, had only been king for a short time before his marriage to Henrietta. The marriage had been arranged for political and strategic reasons binding France and England together. As part of the agreement, Henrietta was allowed to follow her Catholic religion, even though the British monarchy had adopted Protestantism as the nation's official religion.

As Charles and Henrietta's love grew, an understanding and respect for each other developed outside of the obligations to their respective countries. Their happiness was sealed when Henrietta knew she was expecting her first baby. Unfortunately, the baby was born prematurely and did not survive. She was devastated at the loss of her baby and decided to recuperate in the beautiful countryside of Kent, taking solace at the spa that had been discovered 20 years earlier by Lord North.

Lord North had been visiting his friend, Lord Abergavenny, at his hunting lodge in Eridge. As he traveled back to London, he noticed some strange water seeping up from the ground. It had the same iron-tinted waters as he remembered of the Chalybeate Spa on the continent, and he was intrigued. He knelt down and rubbed his fingers through the water and touched them to his lips. The taste was distinctive and he knew immediately he had discovered a natural spring. There were no buildings around except a little shack where a woman emerged with a bowl so that North could taste the water. He collected a small sample of the water and took it to London for analysis. His instincts had been correct, the water showed high levels of sodium chloride, calcium sulfate, ferrous carbonate and many other minerals.

In the years that followed, word spread quickly about the healing powers of the spring. Mrs. Humphreys, the lady who had first given a bowl to Lord North to sample the spring, lived until she was 102. Lord North also had a long and healthy life, living until he was well into his 80th year. He credited the spring with his longevity and soon it became a well-known landmark and pilgrimage for the sick and ailing.

After the loss of her first baby in 1629, Henrietta and her entourage decided to visit the spring in an attempt to help restore the Queen's health and spirits. It had been over 20 years since the discovery by North, but there were no buildings or any permanent structures on the site. Henrietta's group erected tents and planned to camp there for six weeks to take solace in the waters, but her health improved so quickly that she felt the need to see her beloved king. She cut her convalescence short and left "suddenly by great journeys" to Oatlands where King Charles was waiting. Their reunion was rewarded with

Charles II who was often reminded when he was older, "Remember you are the fruit of our love."

As Henrietta and Charles' love grew, so did her influence over him. She wielded it often for her benefit and that of her consorts, but she also began advising the king on matters of state. Many in court felt that she flaunted her Catholic teachings and insisted on having huge numbers of courtiers being favored by the king and members of Parliament.

After many turbulent years, the religious and economic situation worsened in England, providing a fertile ground for civil war. Charles believed in the ultimate rule of the monarch and often clashed with Parliament by taking advice from Henrietta that was ill advised. The climax came in 1648 when Charles tried to have five members of Parliament arrested because they opposed his rule. He was put on trial for treason, found guilty and sentenced to death. Henrietta fought desperately to save his life but it was in vain. He was beheaded on January 30, 1649, and it is said he wore two shirts on that faithful day so the people who witnessed his execution would not see his body tremble. It is also reputed that the last thing he said was "remember."

Even today, many people still do "remember" King Charles I on the anniversary of his death by dressing in 17th-century costumes and parading to the spot where he lost his head.

## What to see and do today:
### The Pantiles
After the visit by Queen Henrietta to the spring in 1629, a book was written by Dr. Rowzee called "The Queen's

Wells," telling of the healing powers of the waters. There was supposedly an influx of visitors and this is believed to be what finally put Royal Tunbridge Wells on the map.

The area around the famous well is now called The Pantiles. There are many towns that claim to have pedestrian precincts but only Royal Tunbridge Wells has one that was truly laid out in the Stuart fashion. The name of the district is derived from the extensive use of square clay tiles, called "pantiles," used to surface the area.

Over the years many celebrities have performed at the spring. Nell Gwyn, a London girl, stole the heart of King Charles II when she performed her reputedly brash and bawdy repartee. Nell later gave birth to a boy who was said to be the illegitimate son of Charles. The king recognized the boy as his own and supported Nell and her son for the rest of his life. Another relationship developed between Peg Huges, a similar entertainer and Prince Albert, although there is no evidence of offspring. The association between royalty and stage performers would continue for centuries, much to the annoyance of monarchs like Queen Victoria.

**The Church of King Charles the Martyr**
The church of King Charles the Martyr was built in 1678 and is quite different from other churches because of the magnificent plaster ceiling and decorative oak-paneled benches. There are guided tours plus lunchtime concerts and recitals.
Telephone: (0) 1892 525455. Address: Located behind the spring.

**The Museum and Art Gallery**
The museum has fine displays of historical costumes, dolls, toys and natural history. The art gallery sometimes shows exhibits from major British and European muse-

ums as well as famous works of art from local and national artists.
Telephone: (0) 1892 545449. Address: Civic Centre, Mount Pleasant, Royal Tunbridge Wells.

**Spa Valley Railway**
A great way to see the countryside of Kent and visit Groombridge and the Enchanted Forest. The steam train travels about three miles, stopping at High Rocks, and continues to Groombridge.
Telephone: (0) 1892 537715. Address: West Station, Royal Tunbridge Wells.

## For more information:
Telephone: (0) 1892 515675. Address: The Old Fish Market, The Pantiles, Royal Tunbridge Wells.

## Food for thought:
**The Brokers Arms**
The Brokers Arms began life as a coaching inn called The White Hart when it was built in 1620. The inn serves the finest pedigree real ales available, and the landlord boasts "you won't find better anywhere in England." There is a resident chef who prides himself on his meat, poultry and fish dishes. Vegetarian meals are also a specialty.
Telephone: (0) 1892 541000. Address: 5-11 Langton Road, Royal Tunbridge Wells.

## If you decide to stay:
**The Swan Hotel**
Located right in the middle of the Pantiles, the hotel is close to all amenities and offers a full restaurant and bar. The restaurant is designed on the Palm Court design — open and full of character.

Telephone: (0) 1892 543319. Address: The Pantiles, Royal Tunbridge Wells.

## Neighboring places of interest:
### Groombridge
The village of Groombridge is located about 3 miles west of Royal Tunbridge Wells. The village grew around a small chapel built by John Packer about 1625. It is reputed that he did not agree with King James I's intentions of building new alliances with Spain. King James sent his son Prince Charles, and an escort, the Duke of Buckingham, to Spain to arrange a marriage with Infanta, a Spanish princess. After six months of traveling, the prince returned unsuccessful. It is said that John Packer was so happy the union did not take place, he put a tablet on the porch of his chapel stating his feelings.

The Walks, as they are called in Groombridge, are a delightful row of 18th-century cottages that line the triangular village green. The cobbled street and pretty houses with weather boarding and hung tiles are distinctly Kentish architecture.

### The Enchanted Forest and Gardens
Beautiful, walled, formal gardens take a visitor back in time to the 17th century because much of the gardens have been preserved for centuries. The exquisite flowers, trees and shrubs create a wonderful atmosphere and, as the Washington Post reported, "It is a fascinating work of art in progress."

### Canal Boat Rides
The canal boats are spacious and comfortable and offer a rare insight into the surrounding countryside that cannot usually be seen. The boatmen give a detailed account of the gardens and the history of the area.

Telephone: (0) 1892 863999. Address: Groombridge Place, Groombridge.

## Food for thought:
### The Crown Inn
The Crown Inn is under new management, and is located on the Wealden Way, which comprises about 80 miles of walking and hiking paths across Kent. The inn was originally built in the 16th century as a coaching facility and has retained much of its character with exposed wooden beams, inglenook fireplaces and low ceilings. They offer an extensive à la Carte menu and traditional pub food. The beer is cask conditioned and is considered by the locals "as the best in the neighborhood." There are four guest bedrooms available that are decorated tastefully with the visitor's comfort in mind.
Telephone: (0) 1892 864742. Address: The Green, Groombridge.

## How to get there:
There is regular direct train service from London Bridge to Tunbridge Wells.

**By car**: Head south or southeast from London to M25. Exit at junction 5 and take A21 to Tunbridge Wells. Leave A21 at the junction with A26. Turn left onto A26 and pass through the roundabout and turn left onto Linden Park Road and then left again onto The Pantiles. Tunbridge Wells is approximately 39 miles away from central London.

# Westerham

John Fryth was called a "obstinate heretic" by the bishops of London for refusing to recant his views, and was condemned to death by burning at the stake. As the faggots were lit, he proclaimed his commitment in his translation of the Bible from Latin to English. His greatest wish was to interpret the language in a form that the average man could read and enjoy with his family. He died by fire at Smithfield, London, on July 4th 1533, still clinging to his beliefs.

Fryth was born in Westerham in 1503. His parents had little money, and they struggled to provide a good life for themselves and their son. They were determined he should have the best education they could afford, and sent John to Eton and then on to King's College, Cambridge. He proved to be a talented student, well liked by his peers and soon caught the attention of Cardinal Wolsey who saw potential in the young man. After his education at Cambridge, Fryth was offered a position as junior canon at Cardinal College, Oxford.

Fryth continued to work hard at the college and showed a pleasant, willing disposition. He was regarded highly by his peers and made many friends including William Tyndale, an ordained priest who was in the process of translating the Bible from Latin to English. Fryth was intrigued by the concept and offered to work with Tyndale as his assistant. There were many priests who were skeptical about the work but the two young men had found a common goal and they were excited by the challenge and unaware of potential dangers.

Tyndale and Fryth worked tirelessly and were so engrossed in their translation, they were unaware that many bishops found their work disturbing and bordering on heresy. The two men were reprimanded and advised to stop work immediately, but they would not because they believed they were doing God's work. Fryth was promptly locked in the college's fish cellar as punishment, but he still continued to write. Finally, he was released on the understanding he would only work on those duties given him by the bishops and stay close to the college. Since he was a headstrong young man, he did not abide by their rules and decided to the leave the country. He moved to Antwerp and taught school at the University of Marburg. In 1528, when he was about 25 years old, he married a local girl and soon began a family.

Living away from England was hard on Fryth. He made little money from his teaching position and he wanted to return to England with his new wife and children. Upon learning of Fryth's desire to return, King Henry VIII suggested that a proposal be drawn up stating certain conditions of entry. Fryth was excited about the plan but when he read the conditions that stated he renounce all previous views and opinions, he became so angry that he wrote a paper against the principles of purgatory and remained in exile. However, in 1532, Fryth received the news that his friend and mentor Tyndale had been arrested on a charge of heresy. He decided to risk everything and return to England to help his friend.

On Fryth's arrival in England he met with the Prior of Reading, who listened sympathetically to his claims of persecution. Ultimately, however, the prior had Fryth arrested and locked in the stocks, where he was pelted with rotten fruit and vegetables. Soon after the punishment in the stocks, Sir Thomas More issued a warrant for Fryth's arrest and, although he tried desperately to escape, he was captured and taken to the Tower of London.

While Fryth was imprisoned at the Tower, he produced some of his finest works. The prison keeper was a kind and sympathetic man who often allowed Fryth to leave for short periods of time so that he could "consult with other godly men." While imprisoned, he developed a formula for the principles of the sacrament of Holy Communion, which was later used as the official doctrine of the Church of England. During his time in the Tower, he was given ample opportunity to renounce his views and opinions but each time he refused to cooperate. He was eventually tried for heresy before the Bishops of London, Winchester and Chichester. He was pronounced guilty as charged and sentenced to death. Fryth was adamant to the end and worked literally until the last minute of his life before he was taken to the stake and put to death.

William Tyndale continued his life's ambition of providing a bible in English, but this time under the watchful eyes of the bishops. At one meeting with other clergymen it is said that Tyndale became so angry that he thumped his fist on the table and said, "If God spare my life, ere many years I will cause a boy that driveth the plough to know more of the Scriptures than thou dost."

In 1536, Tyndale was aware that time was running out because the bishops constantly criticized his work and openly argued with his interpretation. It had been 3 years since Fryth had been burned at the stake and although the church had tried various tactics to control Tyndale, he continued to work in a manner that was unacceptable to the bishops. Finally they decided to put an end to his work altogether and recruited a "friend" of Tyndale called Henry Phillips to assist them with their plan. Phillips helped to incriminate Tyndale and also arranged to be at a specific location where soldiers waited to arrest him. As they walked to the dreaded meeting, Phillips took advantage of Tyndale and borrowed 40 shillings from him knowing he would not have to repay the debt. Tyndale was arrested, tried for heresy and sentenced to death at the stake. The executioner strangled Tyndale as an act of compassion before the fire was lit. He died on October 6, 1536. His last words as documented by a contemporary, John Foxe, were, "Lord, open the King of England's eyes."

**The Wilberforce Oak Tree (or Slave Tree)**
In 1788, an unusual and important meeting took place under an ancient oak tree in Westerham. William Pitt the Younger, Prime Minister of England, and William Wilberforce, a Member of Parliament, sat and discussed the awful practice of slave trading. Unsure of the opposition in Parliament, the two decided on a plan and Wilberforce made a pledge when he "vowed to rid the world of this hideous trade of slavery."

A Bill was drawn up abolishing the slave trade and immediately presented to the House of Commons. The slave trade provided an abundance of wealth to many influential families and Wilberforce suspected the bill to be challenged in parliament. To his surprise, the act was passed in 1789 but the terrible slave trade continued for another 20 years with awful atrocities at sea. Naval patrols guarded the Ivory Coast in an attempt to control the situation, and it is known that the captains of vessels tossed their human cargoes overboard in an attempt to avoid inspection and arrest.

Wilberforce gained many enemies because of his stand against slavery. He felt as though his life was in danger and reverted to having an armed guard accompany him for the rest of his days.

The fine oak tree that Wilberforce and Pitt sat beneath when they discussed the slave trade lasted for centuries but perished during WWII. However, another was planted in the hollow remains to honor the two men and their courageous stand.

A memorial bench with its inscription is located about 4 miles from north of Westerham. It is not easy to find but the monument is important. It can be found just before the village of Keston, at the end of the village in Leaves Green. Take the A233 London Road from Westerham towards Biggin Hill (the most famous Battle of Britain fighter station), continue past the aerodrome to Leaves Green and then take a right turn at the mini roundabout at Downes Road. There is a Boy Scout camp just on the left-hand side of the road, called Wilberforce Camp, and if one continues past this along Downes Road for half a mile, also on the left, there is a local signpost, footpath to Keston (1 mile). Along this one finds a ramblers' sign post, Farnborough Circular walk, and this leads to the Wilberforce Tree monument. The tree is located approximately 400 yards from the road junction immediately south of Keston Ponds.

The inscription reads:

*Mr. Wilberforce's diary, 1787*
*At length I remember after a conversation with Mr. Pitt in the open air at the root of an old tree at Holwood just above the steep descent into the vale of Keston we resolved to give notice on a first occasion in the House of Commons of my intention to bring forward the abolition of the slave trade. Erected by Earl Stanhope, 1862.*

## What to see and do today:
The town of Westerham appears in the Domesday Book survey of 1086 as Oistreham and has always been an important coaching stop for travelers on their way from London to the coast of Kent.

The famous General James Wolfe was born in Westerham on January 2, 1727. He became a highly decorated soldier who fought and lost his life in Québec, Canada, after capturing Québec for England. He defeated the French who were under the command of Marquis de Montcalm and gained Canada for the British. He lived in Québec House, which is now under guardianship of the National Trust. There is a wonderful statue of Wolfe in the center of the town, sword held aloft as though charging into battle.

### Squerryes Court
Squerryes Court is a magnificent, privately-owned manor built in 1681. The Warde family acquired the home in 1731, and it is still owned and occupied by the same family today. The home has a fine selection of paintings by the Old Masters, as well as porcelain and tapestries that were collected by the Warde family in the 18th century. The beautifully landscaped gardens have a variety of carefully planted flowers so there is always something in bloom. There is also a topiary and an 18th-century dovecote in the gardens.

Homemade teas are served in the Old Library at Squerryes Court from 2:00 until 5:00 p.m. on the days the manor house is open to the public.

Open: April 1 until September 30. From 12:00 noon until 5:30 p.m. Wednesday, Saturday and Sunday only. Telephone: (0) 1959 562345. Address: Westerham.

# Food for thought:
## The Grasshopper Inn
The Grasshopper Inn combines 13th-century charm with 20th-century atmosphere, comfort and amenities. It is believed that John Fryth's father was once a landlord of the Grasshopper Inn. The inn derives its name from the heraldic crest of the ancient Gresham family who had a county seat at Titsey, about 2 miles from Westerham. For many years the Grasshopper Inn was a coaching station, and was the boarding point for the coach service that traveled daily between Westerham and Fleet Street.

The inn caters to individuals and large groups for breakfast, morning coffee, lunch and dinner. The Carvery (a selection of roast meat) is considered the best in the area by the local people. Roast beef and turkey is carved to order and served with all the trimmings such as Yorkshire puddings, roast potatoes and fresh vegetables. A beer garden with great views of the countryside is also available. Telephone: (0) 1959 563136. Address: Westerham Road (A25) about ½ mile from the town.

# If you decide to stay:
## Kings Arms Hotel
The hotel was built in 1889 as an elegant coaching inn and is located in the middle of the town. It has a warm, Old-World feeling resembling a Gentlemen's Club with a quiet and calm atmosphere. The menu in the bar and restaurant are extensive and not expensive. The hotel is mentioned in the "Old English Inns" handbook and has a total of 17 guest rooms individually designed and named with a specific theme in mind. The bedrooms have tea and coffee facilities and many of the rooms have splendid four-poster beds with soft, comfortable furnishings.

Telephone: (0) 1959 562990. Address: High Street, Westerham.

## Neighboring place of interest:
### Chartwell House

Chartwell House, the home of Winston Churchill for over 40 years, bears the love and consideration of the famous man. The gardens and beautiful lake, where black swans still adorn the quiet and peaceful countryside, are where Churchill contemplated England's future. Many of his paintings, photographs and mementos can be seen in his studio. Churchill purchased the house in 1920 in poor condition for around 5,000 pound sterling. It is said that Churchill's wife used to sit with an umbrella held over her head because the roof leaked in places, but renovations were underway quickly. On a section of the wall surrounding the garden, there is a plaque stating "The greater part of this wall was built between the years 1925–32 by Winston with his own hands." He was known to be difficult at times but also had a good sense of humor. On personal letters, he often put the symbol of a pig because, "a cat will look down on you; a dog will look up to you, but a pig will look you squarely in the eye as an equal."

The peaceful and quiet garden was a special place for Churchill. He would sit for hours enjoying the solitude and writing his speeches, even possibly his most famous to the nation during WWII, "...we shall not flag nor fail...we shall go on to the end...but we shall never surrender..."

There is a restaurant in the grounds serving a variety of meals from a light snack to more substantial meals. There is plenty of room for parking and many places to sit and have a packed lunch.

Open: From April 1 until October 31, from 11:00 a.m. until 5:00 p.m., Wednesday, Thursday, Friday, Saturday and Sunday. Also open Tuesdays in July and August. Telephone: (0) 1732 866868. Address: Chartwell, Westerham.

## How to get there:
There is no direct train service from London to Westerham; however, it is possible to take a train from London Victoria to Oxted, which is about 5 miles from Westerham. **By car**: Head southeast from London on A20/M20 to M25. Take the M25 south and exit at junction 5 onto A21. Exit A21 onto A25 heading west towards Westerham for about 2 miles. Turn right onto A233 into Westerham village. Westerham is approximately 25 miles away from central London.

*Winston Churchill at Chartwell*

# Ightham Mote

The moated manor house was built in 1330 with additions through 1500. It survived during Oliver Cromwell's time only because his troops could not locate it and so raided another house instead. Believed to be one of the best-preserved medieval houses in the country, it has been the home to many important people although none have been royalty. In approximately 1346, Robert Cawne, who fought alongside the Black Prince at Crècy, France, inherited the home from his father, Sir Thomas Cawne. During Elizabeth I's reign, the Lord Mayor of London hid his Catholic wife at Ightham Mote in an attempt to protect her from the Protestant queen. Finally, the last owner of the home was an American who purchased the home during the 1950s.

Sir Thomas Cawne died in 1374 and willed the home to his son Robert. Sir Thomas was a brave and honorable man and Robert constantly aspired to meet his father's approval. When an opportunity arose for him to join King Edward III and his son, the Black Prince, on the battlefield, Robert was overjoyed. The Black Prince was known to be an expert with a sword and also a skilled horseman. His name is thought to have derived from the black armor he wore into battle, which must have seemed particularly intimidating. The conflict was at Crècy, France, where the King of France waited with thousands of knights and as many foot soldiers. But the English king had a new and formidable weapon, the English longbow. In the right hands, it was capable of providing such power that its arrows could pass through chain mail. The battle at Crècy was over quickly as approximately 4,000 knights and as many foot soldiers fell under the waves of arrows from the longbows and were then finished off with swords and axes.

Ten years later on September 19, 1356, another battle between the French and English at Poitiers took a disastrous turn for the English army. The French force of 20,000 troops vastly outnumbered the 4,000 English soldiers. The Black Prince, seeing the uselessness of the situation, offered to surrender and therefore save his soldiers' lives. Remembering the slaughter by the British at Crècy, the King of France refused their plea. Once the negotiations had failed, the Black Prince ordered his men to fight to their death believing they had nothing to lose. To his surprise and that of the King of France, the French were defeated. The king was taken prisoner and transported to the Tower of London where a ransom of 3 million crowns was demanded for his safe return to France. The ransom was paid and King John was returned to France unharmed.

The Black Prince did not become King of England and died on June 8, 1376, at 46 years of age. His prowess on the battlefield was inherited from his father Edward III and great grandfather Edward I, rather than his grandfather, Edward II who was a weak and ineffectual king. After Robert the Bruce's victory over King Edward II he stated, "I am more afraid of the bones of the father dead, than of the living son; and, by all the saints, it was more difficult to get half a foot of the land from the old king than a whole kingdom from the son!"

Edward I was a great king whose military excellence was recognized and feared by his enemies. He had a hot temper and realized early in his career this was something he needed to control. At 25 years of age, he led the charge into battle at Lewes in East Sussex, and was so overwhelmed with excitement, he carelessly pursued soldiers while his father was outflanked by the enemy and had to surrender. He never forgot this lesson and went on to be one of the mightiest warrior kings of England.

The last owner of Ightham Mote was an American called Charles Henry Robinson. Robinson first saw the home as he cycled around the countryside and fell in love with it. When the home came on the market years later, he purchased it with every good intention of making it his permanent home but the refurbishment was costly. He died in 1985 and left it to the National Trust. During recent renovations, shoes have been found in the walls at the mote. They were usually placed at the weakest point of entry such as above fireplaces, doorways and under the stairs. The intent was to keep evil spirits from entering the house. This practice continued for centuries as can be seen from the shoes on display at the manor.

## What to see and do today:

The Saxon name for Ightham was Ehteham. The splendid, romantic manor has been restored over the centuries using Kentish ragstone, enabling the buildings to keep their medieval appearance. It is believed to be one of the best-preserved homes in the country. Entry to the home is across a stone bridge. There is a medieval "letter box" of sorts on the left-hand side of the entrance. Its purpose is obvious and enabled servants to pass documents on to the current owner. The great hall was the original building while the other followed and formed the quadrangle we see today.

William Jackson Palmer, a famous railway promoter and one of the founders of Colorado Springs, Colorado, rented the property around 1886. Palmer and his wife Mary (Queen) entertained many important guests at the manor such as novelist Henry James and the famous painter, John Singer Sargent. A painting on display at the manor is called "Young lady in white". The young woman in the painting is Elsie Palmer. Elsie is also included in another painting titled "A game of bowls, Ightham Mote."

Another fine painting displayed in the manor is of Lady Dorothy Selby in 1578. It seems the lady died of an infection after pricking her finger. It is the custom to leave a light on in the tower so the ghost of Lady Dorothy does not haunt the manor.

There is a wonderful exhibit of shoes that have been excavated from the buildings dating from 1600 to 1800. As mentioned, it was common practice during medieval times to place shoes in strategic places of entry such as doors, windows and chimneys to keep evil spirits from entering the house. Shoes were used because the builders believed they retained the shape and therefore the spirit of the owner and were consequently symbolic objects. The origin of this practice may have been the "Builders Sacrifice." This involved placing human sacrifices in the walls of important buildings with the intent to ward off bad spirits. Over the centuries, the awful practice of human sacrifice was replaced with animals and then finally shoes. The collection of shoes at the manor shows how long this custom continued.

Open: April 1 through November 1, from 11:00 a.m. until 5:30 p.m. Not open Tuesday and Saturday.
Telephone: (0) 1732 810378. Address: Ivy Hatch, Sevenoaks.

*Ightham Mote*

## Food for thought:
### The Plough Pub
The Plough Pub is less than one mile from Ightham Mote and is well known by the locals and visitors for the variety of meals on the menu. Seafood dishes such as home potted shrimp, fresh oysters and sweet marinated anchovies are available, as are such treats as bacon and mushroom tart and game casserole. A menu is also available for vegetarian meals.
Telephone: (0) 1732 810268. Address: High Cross Road, Ivy Hatch.

## If you decide to stay:
### Rosewood B&B
Rosewood bed and breakfast is located within a few miles of Ightham Mote and 45 minutes from Gatwick Airport. The rooms at Rosewood are attractively decorated and guests can relax in their own comfortable lounge and din-

ing room. Sevenoaks railway station is 15 minutes' drive with services to London that take about 30 minutes.

**The Royal Oak Hotel**
The Royal Oak Hotel is located in a perfect place to discover Kent, which is also known as The Garden of England. It was built in the 18th century of Kentish ragstone and was originally a coaching inn. There are 37 rooms with bathrooms en suite, each with coffee and tea making facilities. A licensed bar and restaurant are on the first floor.
Telephone: (0) 1732 451109. Address: High Street, Sevenoaks.

## Neighboring places of interest:
### Knole
This magnificent home is the largest private house is England. The house is comprised of approximately 4 acres of Kentish stone and is incredible in size. The name was given to the house because of the location set on a rounded hill or knoll. It appears as if it were a castle with its battlement towers, gables and turrets.

Knole was first referred to in 1291, although it was not until around 1456 that its history is better documented. In 1538, King Henry VIII took possession and spent a considerable amount of money in refurbishment and additions. Queen Elizabeth gave Knole to her cousin Thomas Sackville in 1603.

The immense size of the home is astonishing. Instead of only one long gallery, as is common in Elizabethan homes, Knole has three galleries with state bedrooms attached. These are decorated with beautiful furnishing using brocades, velvets and silks. The house is especially known for its exhibition of Elizabethan and Jacobean furniture, paintings and textiles. Over 300 artisans from Italy were brought to Knole to work on specialized masonry, plasterwork, glazing and upholstering at a cost of 40,000 pounds sterling.

Open: April 1 through November 1. Noon until 4:00, Wednesday, Thursday, Friday and Saturday. Sunday - 11:00 a.m. until 5:00 p.m.
Telephone: (0) 1732 462100 or 450608. Address: Sevenoaks.

## How to get there:

There is no direct train service from London to Ightham; however, it is possible to take a train from London Victoria to Borough Green, which is only 1 mile from Ightham.
**By car**: Head southeast from London on A20/M20 to Maidstone. Exit at junction 2 and take A227 south to Borough Green and then Ightham. Ightham is approximately 28 miles away from central London.

# Rochester

He seemed to observe the most unusual character traits and subtle idiosyncrasies in everyday people and re-create them in his novels. Charles Dickens, arguably one of the most gifted authors of the 19th century, loved the city of Rochester, the cathedral, the Medway and the castle so much he made the town his permanent home. He lived happily at Gad's Hill Place, a beautiful home that he admired as a young boy and said as much to his father who remarked, "…if you were to be very persevering and were to work hard you might someday come to live in it." It was at Gad's Hill that he wrote many of his most famous works including *Pickwick Papers* and *Great Expectations,* using specific places in Rochester as the setting. A favorite pastime of Dickens was to sit quietly in a small graveyard across the road from the cathedral and think about his manuscripts. One day, as he was sitting with a friend, he pointed to the cathedral and said, "There, my boy, I mean to go into dust and ashes." Unfortunately, his wishes were not granted and he was buried in Westminster Abbey.

Charles Dickens was born in Portsmouth on February 7, 1812. He was the second child and the first son of six children born to Elizabeth and John. Their third child Letitia died in infancy. Charles was a sickly child with a delicate constitution and would rather stay indoors reading while his siblings played outside. He was a voracious reader and would take his father's books from the attic and read them one after the other.

The Dickens family moved from Portsmouth to Chatham and then to Camden Town, London, where they leased a small cottage. Dickens' father was unsuccessful in his career choices and moved from one job to another. As he did so, the family's economic situation worsened and became so critical that young Dickens was sent to a pawnbroker's shop to sell the family's meager belongings. When he was twelve, he took a job in a blacking factory whose products were used to blacken stoves and pipes. It was dirty, hard work with long hours but he considered himself lucky as children half his age were in workhouses suffering horribly. He tried to blend with the other workers in the factory but he was always different and this showed in his nickname: "the little gentleman."

As Dickens worked in London, he became familiar with many of the less desirable places such as Limehouse and the East India Docks. These were generally considered dens of inequity and here he rubbed shoulders with many characters with more than a touch of larceny in their hearts. He observed these scoundrels at work and play, and while he did so he noted their harsh language and behavior. He had a wonderful, retentive memory and stored the behavioral details of individuals for future use as the basis of characters in his stories. It is believed his experience working in the blacking factory and observation of underworld life in the East End sparked the idea for *Oliver Twist* with characters such as Bill Sikes, Fagin and his gang.

When Dickens was about 8 years old he was taken to see Grimaldi at the Theatre Royal on Star Hill, Rochester, (now the Conservative Club) and loved the performance.

This seems to have affected him greatly, because he and his elder sister Fanny would perform short plays and skits for the family in the evenings. They also recruited several friends to help them with different characters. Mrs. Godfrey, a sister of the tutor at Dickens' school remarked of Dickens that "...he was a very handsome boy, with long curly hair of a light colour, and that he was of a very amiable, agreeable disposition."

Although Dickens loved to perform, he decided to pursue a career as a reporter and taught himself shorthand relatively quickly. He sent an inquiry letter to the Morning Chronicle and suggested a series called "Sketches of London" in which he would write under the name of Boz. He was accepted and the series proved so successful that it was carried in the Morning and Evening Chronicles. This led to other assignments and gave him the confidence to ask for the hand of Catherine Hogarth in marriage. Catherine was 20 years of age when he proposed; he had known her and her family for many years.

Dickens married Catherine on April 2nd 1836, at St. Lukes Church, Chelsea, and they honeymooned for two weeks at Chalk, a small town about 5 miles from Rochester. He continued to work despite their honeymoon because "the publishers will be here in he morning." Now a journalist with the Morning Chronicle, he was providing high quality work, some of which was humorous in nature. His mastery of shorthand helped in his work and he was soon in great demand outside of the newspaper assignments. Although he did not let the popularity of his series affect him, he did take an interest in fine clothes and sometimes his waistcoats could be described as gaudy and a little outlandish as was mentioned in the reviews when he visited America.

In November 1838, Dickens had successes far beyond his dreams. He had three young children and a relatively happy family life, although there had been some disturbing comments to friends about his marriage. He decided to spread his wings and visit America, taking with him his wife and her maid, Anne. They left on January 4, 1842, on the first transatlantic steamer, the *Britannia,* under the direction of Captain John Hewitt. The visit to America had been at the suggestion of Messrs. Chapman and Hall who agreed to publish an account of his experiences. The voyage across the Atlantic was a rough one by all accounts and the visit did not go as well as Dickens had planned. He criticized the American audiences for being too sensitive and thin skinned. He described the English audience as "being able to laugh at themselves and having such thick skins that I can almost say almost anything to them." He also had issue with the copyright laws in America and was unhappy that he did not benefit directly from his popularity. He was regretful that his visit to America had not gone well and did not return for 25 years.

There had been many rumors about the Dickens' unhappy marriage for years but they put their differences aside for the sake of the children. In 1858, when the children were in their teens, Catherine and Dickens decided to part and go their separate ways. Dickens was now free of restraints and threw himself wholeheartedly into his work.

On June 9, 1865, after a trip to Europe, Dickens was on a train traveling from Folkstone to London when a freak accident caused the train he was riding in to crash, sending the first 6 carriages over a bridge. Dickens was located in the 7th carriage and was badly shaken but otherwise unhurt. He aided the railway personnel with the dead and dying and this must have affected him greatly because he mentioned years later that he often had "sudden vague rushes of terror, even when riding in a hansom cab."

Dickens was at the height of his popularity and was reading to audiences worldwide. In 1867, he decided on another trip to America and was greatly rewarded with "sold out" performances with more people outside than inside the theatre. The wonderful reviews he obtained from his readings only piqued more interest, which led to an expanded tour. He stayed in the States for 5 months and received 25,000 pounds sterling for his visit, and was even invited to the White House on his birthday. However, his health was failing fast and he often needed help as he mounted the steps to the stage. His heart and leg were giving him considerable pain, making performances difficult. Speaking at his last meeting he said "...I have been received with unsurpassable politeness, delicacy, sweet temper, hospitality...than these two great nations, each of which has its own way and hour striven so hard and so successfully for freedom, ever again being arrayed, the one against the other." He exited the stage under great applause with the help of assistants and was in obvious pain.

Dickens' health continued to deteriorate and at one of the last readings he gave, he mispronounced several words and recognized that he had done so with a slight smile to his family who was sitting in the front row. His inability to express his works eloquently led some to believe he had suffered a slight stroke. He continued to write until he died but did not finish his last manuscript, *The Mystery of Edwin Drood*, even though he worked on it the day before he passed away. At dinner on the night of June 8th, 1870, he seemed disorientated and confessed to "being unwell during the afternoon." A dinner guest suggested that he lay down and rest to which he replied, "Yes, on the ground" and, as he rose to his feet, he staggered and fell. He died the following day, 5 years to the day after the train accident.

Dickens declared in his will that "no special monument, memorial or testimonial should be in my name...that an inexpensive, unostentatious funeral be performed and no reference such as Mr. or Esquire be added on my tomb." The final resting place was Westminster Abbey next to other notable authors such as Shakespeare and Chaucer, but as requested by Dickens, the funeral service was quiet and dignified and his marker simply states in Roman script: Charles Dickens. Born February the Seventh, 1812. Died June the Ninth 1870.

## What to see and do today:

Dickens mentioned several houses in his novels that were based on specific houses in Rochester. The Royal Victoria and Bull Hotel is mentioned in the early chapters of *Pickwick Papers*, Satis House in *Great Expectations* and Rochester Cathedral in the *Mystery of Edwin Drood*. Each year, the town features a Dickens' Day where local people dress in the character of Dickens' novels and there are many festivities.

### Charles Dickens' Museum

His life and works are displayed in The Charles Dickens' Center, known as Eastgate House. The exhibition shows a timeline of Dickens' life and works complete with lifelike waxwork figures of Dickens, Fagin, Sikes, David Copperfield, Oliver Twist and many other characters from his novels. The exhibition also includes great audio and lighting displays.

Open: April to September, 10:00 a.m. until 6:00 p.m. October to March, 10:00 a.m. until 4:00 p.m.

Telephone: (0) 1634 844176. Address: Eastgate House, High Street, Rochester.

**Rochester Cathedral**
A Norman monk called Gundulf built the nave in 1080. It is impressive with its huge pillars; some have carvings on them in the form of faces, a boat and an eagle. The cathedral has seen many additions over the centuries. In 1179, a fire destroyed much of the cathedral and when the monks rebuilt it, they used the Early English style in the arches. Unfortunately money ran out before they reached the nave, and this is the reason there are still many Norman (rounded) arches in the church. There have been so many pilgrimages to the cathedral that the flagstones are worn away in places. It is believed that William of Perth, a baker who was on a pilgrimage in 1201, stopped at Rochester overnight but was murdered. His murderer was never found but his body was taken to the cathedral where it was buried. After the burial, it is said that miracles took place and people were healed of their terrible afflictions. This further increased the interest by pilgrims who gave generously to the cathedral and therefore helped with the restoration after the fire.

Brass rubbing is available at the cathedral, but call for specific details. There is also a little tea shop and garden in the cathedral grounds.
Open: Daily from 7:30 a.m. until 6:00 p.m.
(0) 1634 401301. Address: 70a High Street, Rochester.

**Rochester Castle**
The extraordinary Norman arch at the foot of the stairs leading to the castle is intricately and beautifully carved. The Norman masons were well known for their decorative stonework, and the arch fully displays their skill. Once through the gates of the arch, the castle stands majesti-

*Rochester Castle*

cally by the Medway, and one can only imagine the splendor of previous times from the ruins today. The keep is particularly interesting and was added by Henry I around 1126. The walls are approximately 13 feet thick at the base, tapering to about 11 feet at the top. King John laid siege to the castle in 1215 and finally took control after 2 months of fighting. The end came because King John decided to change his strategy. He ordered 40 of the fattest pigs to be taken to the southeast tower, slaughtered and set alight. The ensuing fire caused the tower to collapse and the king's troops were able to enter and take the castle. The tower was rebuilt later in the rounded style we see today.

**The Historic Dockyard**
The paddle steamer *Kingswear Castle* has several trips available including morning, afternoon, evening and full-

day excursions. Dickens often mentioned Chatham Docks, the Medway and many towns along the banks in his novels. This is a good way to see the towns as Dickens saw them.
Open: May to September. Call for specific details.
Telephone: 0 1634 827648. Address: The Historic Dockyard, Chatham.

## Food for thought:
### Ye Olde Curiousitie Tea Shop and Restaurant
The restaurant serves traditional English fare of roast meat, Yorkshire puddings and vegetables as well as steak-and-kidney pies and mashed potatoes. There is a large selection of desserts including treacle tart, spotted dick (a steamed suet pudding with currants) and various fruit pies. Afternoon tea is served with little sandwiches, homemade cakes and biscuits. The restaurant is dated from the 15th century and is said by the proprietor, Denise Sturch, to have a resident ghost. He is a mischievous little fellow who turns faucets on and off and occasionally throws things across the room. One day, as customers watched in amazement, a tablecloth was pulled to the floor with the cutlery crashing to the ground. Was this the naughty boy at play?
Telephone: (0) 1634 840451. Address: 151 High Street, Rochester.

## If you decide to stay:
### Royal Victoria and Bull Hotel
The Royal Victoria is ideally suited for all sightseeing around the town. It is within walking distance of the cathedral, the castle, the Roman ruins and the Dickens Museum. The hotel was originally built as a 16th-century coaching inn and has all the character of bygone days. The guest rooms have bathrooms en suite if needed, with

coffee and teapots, ironing and hair dryer's facilities and a full restaurant. The restaurant has a fully licensed bar and offers a variety of meals including special diet needs.
Telephone: (0) 1634 846266. Address: 16-18 High Street, Rochester.

**Gordon House Hotel**
The hotel was built in the 17$^{th}$ century and has undergone some renovations over the centuries. Recently, some very unusual panels were discovered under some wallpaper in the dining room and these have been preserved as part of the décor. The hotel also boasts of having perhaps the only "hound gate" still in existence. A hound gate was placed at the foot of the stairs and closed at night once the guests were safely tucked in bed. A large hound then stood guard at the gate throughout the night.

The hotel is located close to the cathedral. It has 14 guest rooms all with bathrooms en suite. Tea and coffee facilities are available in all the rooms. There is a licensed bar and a full restaurant for residents only although special consideration is provided for small parties.
Telephone: (0) 1634 831000. Address: 91, High Street, Rochester.

## For more information on Rochester:
Telephone: (0) 1634 843666. Address: 95 High Street, Rochester. Tourist Information Center.

## How to get there:
There is regular direct train service from London Victoria to Rochester.
**By car**: Head southeast from London on A2 east out of London to Rochester. Rochester is approximately 30 miles away from central London.

# Chiddingstone

The village was first mentioned in the Domesday Book in 1086. It is generally believed the village took its name from the Chiding Stone, a large sandstone rock hidden in a meadow where husbands scolded their nagging wives in front of an assembly of villagers. Others believe the name originated from an ancient name like Cedda and gradually changed over the centuries to Chiddingstone.

Chiddingstone is believed to have been settled in prehistoric times because many flints have been unearthed together with large groups of rocks showing natural shelters. Archeological digs have also produced burial urns showing the Romans' presence in the village, and even within the last century people in the village would speak of "Yokes of Chested and Vexour." A yoke is a Roman measurement of land consisting of about 50 acres. Some of these relics are on show at the museum in Royal Tunbridge Wells.

When William the Conqueror invaded England in 1066, he gave much of Kent to his half brother Bishop Odo, and it's thought the village of Chiddingstone became his property as well. The bishop was an ambitious and ruthless man who quickly amassed a fortune and hid it away in Rochester Castle in anticipation of his eventual return to France.

In the 12th century, apart from the Norman invasion, the biggest threat to most villages and towns in England was the Black Death. In 1348, it killed indiscriminately from lords to peasants and, at the end of this year, approximately one-third to one-half of all people in England died. This, in turn, caused a serious shortage of labor that lasted for generations, a situation the peasants did their best to capitalize upon. In 1381, the peasants' revolt started in Brentwood, Essex, and quickly spread to Kent and other counties. It began because a poll tax had been imposed that was almost three times higher than the previous year. This was seen as a diabolical act and the peasants took action.

On June 14th 1381, King Richard II and knights of the realm met with the peasants and their leader, Wat Tyler. History tells us the Kentish peasants behaved well and were pleased the king listened to their grievances. However, Tyler behaved in an arrogant and insolent fashion to the king. The Mayor of London was so incensed by the behavior of Tyler, he pulled him from his horse and had him killed by the guard. Witnessing this, the crowd surged forward but the king calmed them, promising that he would accept their petition and give pardons for those involved in the revolt.

Civil unrest continued in England for many years. The Hundred Years War with France had greatly depleted the country's coffers, and heavy taxes were once more imposed on the people of Britain. They considered the increase unjust because Parliament had mismanaged their financial affairs and were now squeezing money from those least able to afford it. The peasants' rose up again, demanding lower taxes and, as this tax affected everyone, the peasants found themselves supported by the gentry and even some clergymen.

During the year 1450, a mysterious man appeared in Chiddingstone and rallied the militant men in the village to action. Little was known of him; even his name was in dispute. Some knew him as Jack Cade, others said his name was John Mortimer and that he was related to Richard, Duke of York. Some rumored that he took part in the Hundred Years War against England and was now using the rebellion to cause unrest from within Britain.

By all accounts, Cade was a charismatic leader and quickly gained the men's confidence. At least six men from the village, including Roger atte-Wood (one who lives or works near a wood), were ready to fight for their beliefs. Legend has it they met with Cade at the Trugger's farm house and conspired with him to overthrow the king and government.

The unrest in the countryside of Kent continued for months and finally ended in London where the rebels killed the Archbishop of Canterbury, Sir James Fiennes, King Henry's treasurer, and the Sheriff of Kent. They beheaded the archbishop and the treasurer, placed their heads on pikes and paraded them around the city facing each other because as Shakespeare said in his play Henry VI, "...let them kiss one another, for they loved well when they were alive..."

As the fighting continued and the situation worsened, a meeting was arranged between King Henry VI and the rebel leader. The king was acutely aware of the influence of Jack Cade, whose cause had been embraced by the people of London and even some of the king's own soldiers. The king listened to Cade's demands and showed some understanding of the peasants' issues. He commiserated with them and offered pardons to all those involved in the rebellion if they would return to their villages. Cade produced a list of those men and the crowd dispersed feeling as though their battle had been won.

The following day, the king counseled with his advisors and they reconsidered the situation. They determined that no pledge had been made to Cade himself, only the promise of pardons to the peasants, which would be fulfilled. To suppress any further rebellions by Cade, a warrant was issued for this arrest.

The new Sheriff of Kent, Alexander Iden, anxious to avenge the death of his predecessor and prove himself worthy of the position, pursued Cade relentlessly. Cade was finally wounded and captured by Iden and transported back to London. He died during the journey but was still hung, drawn and quartered when he arrived. His head was placed on a pike as was customary for offenses of treason.

## What to see and do today:

Ownership of the buildings in the village have changed often, as can be seen on the deeds. Sir Thomas Bullen (Boleyn), Anne Boleyn's father, purchased the Shop and Old Manor house in 1517, so it is possible Henry courted Anne (and her sister Mary) in the village and Hever castle. Anne never gave Henry the son he so desperately needed but she did give him Elizabeth, who would become a strong and effective Queen.

The village is quite small, consisting of a row of houses, shops and a church that have changed little over the centuries but the whole ambiance is quite beautiful and worthy of a visit.

**The Castle**
The Streatfeild family began their lives as yeoman farmers but their natural business sense took them into the wool and iron industries, both thriving industries where they became very wealthy. They purchased many of the homes adjacent to the castle and gradually developed the park and the lake.

The castle, grounds and lake set in a 3,000-acre estate were built over a 30-year period starting in 1805 by first Henry Streatfeild, and later his son. Denys Bower purchased it in 1955 with intentions of restoring the castle to its previous beauty. Bower, an art dealer, never had quite sufficient funds to complete the project, and the castle fell into disrepair. Eventually a private charity, with the help of the English Heritage, restored the house to its former beauty.
Open: Call for specific days and times.
Telephone: (0) 1892 870347. Address: Chiddingstone Village, Chiddingstone.


**St. Mary's Church**
There has probably been a church on the site of St. Mary's for over a thousand years. The Domesday Book of 1086 mentions a church on this location. It was therefore probably Saxon and made of wood. On July 17, 1624, the church was struck by lightning and caught fire. Some believe the restoration accounts for the different styles that can be seen in the church. In any case, it is a handsome church and shows a fine display of stone faces, which are wonderful examples of the stonemasons' sense of humor. Some carvings are comical and others have large eyes and mouths, some with their tongues out. One shows a double head with two sets of noses and mouths but three eyes.

There are some excellent examples of brasses, iron grave slabs and hatchments in the church. During the reign of King Charles II, the custom of carrying the coat of arms ahead of a funeral procession became fashionable. After the burial, the coat of arms was kept at the church as a sign of appreciation and stature of the family in the community. There is a fine display of these hatchments in St. Mary's church.

### Truggers Farm
Truggers Farm probably got its name from the industry of trug making. Trugs are shallow, rectangle baskets made for collecting produce. This is where it is rumored that Jack Cade met with the villagers and conspired against the Crown.
It is a private residence and is not open to the public.

### The Chiding Stone
A footpath to the Chiding Stone is signposted next to a tiny village green in the High Street. The path has a holly hedge and, depending on the time of year, will be full of red berries and wonderful dark green foliage. The path leads to a "kissing gate" and then onwards to an open area where the large chiding stone can be seen on the right-hand side of the clearing.

## Food for thought:
### The Castle Inn
The Castle Inn has had many names over the years including The Rock House, Waterslip House and the Five Bells. The earliest reference to the inn was in 1420 when it was leased to William Chelsfield for 12 pence. The Castle Inn has an excellent restaurant offering a full menu as well as traditional pub food. The menu offers a variety of dishes and vegetarian meals. There are two well-stocked

*The Chiding Stone*

bars and a beer garden to enjoy a pint on a lovely English summer day.
Telephone: (0) 1892 870247. Address: The Street, Chiddingstone.

## If you decide to stay:
### Larkins Farm
Larkins Farm is a self-catering establishment on the eastern side of the village. It is full of character, with many exposed beams, spacious and comfortable furnishings and wonderful views of the countryside. The Stable has a guest room that sleeps 4 people. The Barn sleeps 7–9 people. There is ample parking and facilities in the village for groceries or the Castle Inn for lunch or dinner.
Telephone: (0) 1732 369168. Address: Chiddingstone. (Properties run by agents: Garden of Eden Cottages numbers 25 and 25A).

# Neighboring places of interest:

### Hever Castle

The huge Gatehouse, outer walls and the moat of Hever Castle were built in 1270. Approximately 200 years later, the beautiful structure we know as Hever Castle was built. It was the childhood home of Anne Boleyn, second wife to Henry VIII. She was unable to give him the son he so desperately needed and the relationship floundered, but it is generally believed that Henry VIII loved Anne and composed *"Greensleeves"* for her. However, once the decision was made to take another as his wife, he abetted those who discredited her by accusing her of adultery and incest, assuring her fate. The Duke of Norfolk, Anne's own uncle, gathered evidence against her and was present along with 2,000 others at her sentencing. Anne's only request was for a skilled executioner to come from Calais, France. He was known to be an expert with a sword and severed her head with one blow. The king was hunting in his favorite place, Epping Forest, at the time of her death and only returned when the gun salute at the Tower of London signaled the deed was complete.

Over the centuries, the castle has been the home of two queens and was well maintained for a long period of time, but for many reasons it fell into disrepair and caused unhappiness to many people. In the early 1900's, an American, William Waldorf Astor, purchased the castle and restored it to its former magnificence, spending literally millions of dollars. Astor's love of the finer things in life can be seen in the castle and the gardens. He had a true sense of history and restored the castle to its former glory. The gardens and maze at Hever Castle are considered among the best in the country. The beautiful costumes, paintings and books in the castle give an idea of what life was like for the young Anne. There are two rare books that

are inscribed and signed by Anne at the castle. One is called "Hours" and was her personal prayer book.
Open: Daily from March 1 until November 30.
Telephone: (0) 1732 865224. Address: Near Edenbridge, Kent.

## How to get there:
There is no direct train or bus service from London to Chiddingstone, however it is possible to take a train from London Bridge to Tonbridge from where Chiddingstone can be reached by taxi. The easiest way to get there is by car.

**By car:** Head southeast from London on A20 to the junction with M25 and turn right onto M25. Take M25 to exit 5 and take A21 south towards Tonbridge. Take the first exit left towards Sevenoaks. Travel just under one-half mile to B2042 and turn right. Head south to B2027 and turn left. Stay on B2027 for about 2 miles and take the road on the right sign-posted for Chiddingstone. Chiddingstone is approximately 30 miles away from central London.

# Pluckley

The Guinness Book of World Records (1998) has Pluckley as being "the most haunted village in the country." There are perhaps 12–16 ghosts that are said to appear in and around the village depending on who is telling the tale, but the village has a rich history beyond the ghosts. At least 50 men from the village participated in the Jack Cade Rebellion of 1450 when the rebels, unhappy with the taxes imposed upon them, met with King Henry VI and their leader, Jack Cade. Most men were later pardoned for their involvement and returned to the village unharmed but others were hung, drawn and quartered. In 1610, two local men, Martin Davye and Thomas Fell had an argument that spilled into the churchyard. Davye struck Fell who later died of his injuries. Davye was charged with murder but claimed "benefit of clergy," which meant that he could read and write Latin and was therefore considered an educated man. Because of this claim, the sentence was reduced to manslaughter.

Pluckley has been the home of many influential and powerful families over the centuries, from the Tilman's who left for America to the Bettenhams and Dering families. The Betttenham and Dering families had a long-standing disagreement concerning the ownership of the coat of arms that was displayed in the church. Each family had a crest depicting a saltire (a x-shaped animal barricade) as the emblem. Both families claimed theirs was the original design and they fought bitterly over the issue for years. Another conflict arose because both families wanted to sit in the most important pew in the church. On one occasion, physical violence broke out between two women from the respective families and Rector John Copley had to intervene.

Church records show that the Dering family was instrumental in the development of the village for centuries. In 1549, Edward Dering was born. He grew into a fine young man and was a gifted student who studied at Cambridge and graduated from Christ's Church in 1560, with a BA and MA. He rose quickly up the ecclesiastical ladder to become Chaplain of the Tower of London. His contemporaries believed that although he had a brilliant, academic mind, he lacked the social graces that were needed in the upper echelons of the church. His puritan views were often considered unorthodox and his plain speaking manner conveyed pointed criticism of his fellow clergymen who did not share his strict Protestant beliefs. Eventually he came to the attention of Queen Elizabeth I for his ardent puritan speeches, and she invited him to address her with a sermon. To the queen's surprise, Dering denounced other clergymen whom he considered unsuitable for the cloth, describing them as "...ruffians, hawkers and dicers..." True to form, Dering also criticized the queen and astounded her courtiers by reprimanding her for her unwillingness to administer justice on these men. He stated, "...in the meanwhile that all these whoredoms are committed, you at whose hands God will require it, you sit still and are careless, and let men do as they will..."

The queen was embarrassed and annoyed at the behavior of Dering in front of her subjects and tried in vain to prevent the minister from preaching in the future. Almost two years later, Dering had to defend himself before the Star Chamber for his writing and preaching of unorthodox ecclesiastical works. He lost his license to preach and died at approximately 36 years of age after succumbing to tuberculosis.

The Star Chamber derived its name from the star pattern design on the ceiling on the chamber at Westminster Palace where the court met. Originally the duties of the Star Chamber were to oversee the more mundane petitions brought before the court during the 15th century. It was not a jury trial but depositions were taken and sentences were dispersed. They consisted mainly of corporal punishment in the form of whippings, time in the stocks and branding. The role of the Star Chamber increased under the Tudors and the Chamber became a favorite political weapon used by King Henry VIII. The court remained in use through the reigns of Elizabeth I, James I and Charles I. The Long Parliament, which initiated discussions to restore the monarchy to full power, dissolved it in 1641.

The legend of the Dering windows that are still seen in the village today originated with a story about a member of the family, a Cavalier, being pursued by Roundhead soldiers. He took refuge in a home where the windows had an unusual shape. The tops of the windows were rounded and this enabled the young man to squeeze through and escape to safety. When he returned home and told his father of his bold adventure, his father was thrilled and suggested the windows in their home should be changed as a tribute to his son's daring feat.

The mystery of haunting in the village and the abundance of ghosts is believed by some to be caused by ley lines. A ley is an ancient track running from one important site to another using various landmarks such as a large stone or "milestone" or a pile of stones "cairn." Sometimes even a group of trees were used to guide a traveler to his destination. Some leys are so distinctive from the air that airplane pilots use them to stay on a particular path or course. It is even said that UFOs have been seen flying along ley lines, attracted in some way by a magnetic force.

There are said to be at least 12–16 ghosts in and around the village of Pluckley. Two of the ghosts are Dering women, one who searches the gravestones looking for her child and the another, a beautiful woman who wears an exquisite gown with a red rose pinned to her bosom. Legend has it her husband placed the rose in the coffin just before it was sealed. He loved his wife deeply and tried to preserve her beauty even in death. He had three lead coffins made each placed inside the other to insure an airtight seal and therefore insulating her beauty forever. However, the story goes that she was as wicked and cruel as she was beautiful.

Other ghosts of the village are the Gypsy Woman who fell asleep while smoking a pipe and died; the poltergeist who moves furniture at The Black Horse Inn and the White Lady of Surrenden Manor. The manor was burned to the ground in 1952, but the previous owner, an American big game hunter, sat up all night waiting for her to appear. Apparently she never did but the game hunter fired a blast of gunshot into the library ceiling for some reason he never explained.

## What to see and do today:
The village is small and consists of some beautiful half-timbered homes and the parish church of St. Nicholas whose foundations date to 1097. The village name is believed to have derived from a Saxon man called Plucca who decided to make the village his home around the 9th century. The village was not mentioned in the Domesday Book of William the Conqueror but was noted in the Domesday Monachorum of the Canterbury monks in

1090. The village lies to the north of the Kentish Weald known for its excellent hiking trails.

### St. Nicholas
St. Nicholas is a splendid old church with the nave and tower dating from around the 13th century. There were renovations during the 14th and 15th centuries in the form of some buttresses and a medieval shingled spire. The area around the font and on the East Side of the aisle has been paved with stones from the graveyard. The notations to the Derings are in much evidence in the church including brasses, coats of arms and inscriptions on the beautifully carved screens.

The church has extensive parish records starting in 1560. During 1631, two rival families, the Derings and Bettenham women fought (literally) for use of a specific pew in the church. The Bettenham and Derings' quarrels landed them in the Star Chamber twice, the King's Bench and four times in the Chancery. It is not known if any resolution came from these proceedings.

## Food for thought:

### The Black Horse
The Black Horse pub was built in 1450 and is within a few yards of the church. The Black Horse was originally a farmhouse that was surrounded by a moat. The pub has its own poltergeist that rearranges the furniture and "hides" things. The pub has been featured in the television series of *"The Darling Buds of May"* starring Catherine Zeta Jones and David Jason. Most people visit the pub for its "good food, fine wine and ales ~ that's all we need…" but others visit in the hopes of seeing the poltergeist at work. Besides the excellent menu, they have special dietary meals available and a great beer garden.

Telephone: (0) 1233 840256. Address: The Street, Pluckley.

**Dering Arms**
The landlord of the Dering Arms specializes in fish and visits the coast many times each week, returning with a variety of catch including lemon sole, lobster, sea bass, etc. Also on the menu are pasta dishes, soups and fresh vegetables most of which come from the owner's farm. The wine list boasts a selection of over 100 while the beer is considered the best in the area. The pub is decorated with garlands of hop vines, and there occasionally is a live band. The inn's three guest rooms have hand basins and tea and coffee appliances, but do not include en suite bathrooms. A substantial English breakfast is included as part of the service. "The emphasis is on good, food, wine/beer and excellent company...and we are located just 100 yards from Pluckley station." Please note there is no food available on Sunday evening and all day Monday.
Telephone: (0) 1233 840371. Address: Station Road, Pluckley.

# If you decide to stay:
## Elvey Farm Country Hotel
The Elvey Farm Hotel is still a working farm but many of the buildings have been renovated for use as guest facilities. The buildings have exterior and interior oak beamed rooms and an unusual type of roof. The tiles for the roof were handmade in the 15th century and are known as "peg tiles." The oast house and barn have been converted into guest rooms, each comprising of three double rooms with bathrooms en suite. The décor is soft and comfortable and in character of the time.

The Dering family, who also owned much of the countryside, once owned the farm. The wonderful woods located close to the farm are now owned by the Woodland Trust and are open to the public. Please be sure to honor the rules of the countryside by closing all gates and leaving only your footprints.

Telephone: (0) 1233 840442. Address: Elvey Lane, located between Pluckley and Edgerton (approximately 2 miles).

## How to get there:

There is direct train service from London Bridge to Pluckley. Allow about 1 hour for the journey.

**By car**: Head southeast from London on A20/M20 towards Ashford. Exit at junction 8 and take A20 east. At about one-half mile after the roundabout junction with A252, turn right at Chegsworth Road and go through Coppins Corner to Pluckley. Pluckley is approximately 54 miles away from central London.

# Chilham

In 1715, a boy called Lancelot Brown was born in Kirkharle, Northumberland. He rose from humble beginnings to become a master landscaper and designer to King George III. His exceptional work at Hampton Court, Blenheim Palace, Chatham and Chilham Castle caused a mild sensation. On hearing of Brown's death in 1783, Sir Horace Walpole, Britain's Prime Minister said, "Such was the effect of his genius that when he was the happiest man he will be least remembered, so closely did he copy nature that his works will be mistaken." Brown often described himself as a "place-maker" not a landscaper, but his use of lakes, trees and Ha-Ha walls provide us with a legacy we enjoy today.

Brown finished school at 16, which was late for those times when children were usually put into service at approximately 12 years of age. He served as an apprentice to Sir William Lorraine, where he learned the art of land reclamation, forestry and horticulture. After living and working in Kent for many years, he finally moved to London where he opened a business in Hammersmith. His company flourished in part because he followed his instincts and love of horticulture to provide landscapes he considered to be typically English. He soon became known as "Capability" Brown because of the phrase "capability for improvement" that he often used when describing the potential of an estate.

The commission for Chilham came in 1777. The estate comprised approximately 300 acres, but it was the area around the mansion that was reworked by Brown. He "molded" the countryside by hiding those things he considered unsightly through the use of terracing, trees and shrubs. The use of Ha-Ha walls became his standard way of keeping deer and other animals from approaching the gardens. They are almost-invisible barriers that provide an uninterrupted view of the landscape. Ha-Ha structures come in three basic designs, but the one most favored by Brown was the Ha-Ha wall. This design is best used where a lawn meets a meadow. A ditch is dug with a vertical side of about 4 feet and the side closest the house is lined with bricks. The ditch has a flat bottom of about 4 feet and then rises gently in a slope until it reaches the top of the meadow. In this fashion, an animal can graze on the slope and bottom of the ditch but is prevented from approaching the house by the brick wall.

During Brown's lifetime, some contemporaries criticized his work, saying that he "butchered" the landscape. However, his work was greatly appreciated by his patrons and this showed in his commissions, which totaled over 200 in 30 years of business. Some of his works were on a massive scale, incorporating thousands of acres. Others were more modest but each showed the "magic" of his touch. His sinuous lakes appear to reflect the sun's rays and his wonderful use of color and texture in trees and shrubs create a brilliant work of art. It is difficult to see where Brown's hand finishes and nature begins, such is the legacy he left us.

There is a legend that began in the 13th century associated with the park at Chilham. It is believed that disaster will befall the owner of the castle if the herons do not nest in the park by Valentine's Day. This type of legend is also attached to the Tower of London, except the birds are ravens and the Ravenmaster trims the birds' wings gently on one side so they cannot escape!

## What to see and do today:
Standing on the old Pilgrim's Way, Chilham has changed little over the centuries. It is the last stage of the pilgrimage route from London to Canterbury, which is only 5 miles to the east of the village.

The square in the village has half-timbered Tudor houses with lattice windows and overhanging upper stories that are so perfect they have been used for many film sets and television series. The red brick buildings at the edge of the square are merely a façade and were originally half timbered, as are the others.

There are some firemarks on the outside of homes in the square. These firemarks were an indication the house was covered by an insurance company's private fire brigade. Sometimes there was more than one insurance company in a village and a brigade was called out for the wrong home. The fire brigade would literally let the house burn to the ground if it was not covered under their company's plan. Competition for business was so fierce that when the legitimate fire brigade appeared on the scene, a fight would break out. The house would literally be burned to the ground while the fireman kicked over each other's leather buckets.

After William the Conqueror invaded England in 1066, he gave the village of Chilham as a prize to his half brother, Bishop Odo. During the 13th century, the village changed hands again and it was given to Richard, the illegitimate son of King John. Richard had been known as Richard Fritzroy, a common name given to illegitimate children of a king. Richard eventually married Rochese de Dover and took her last name as his own.

Sir Dudley Digges built a splendid Jacobean house in the village. Work began in 1603 from the architectural plans of Indigo Jones, a famous English architect, taking 13 years to build. The Digges were an influential family in Chilham, as can be seen from the monument in the church.

An ancient custom has recently been revived that began with the Digges' family in 1638. Sir Dudley Digges, who was a highly ranked official in the court of James I, organized an event called the Young Men and Maidens Race. This race took place during the height of summer and youngsters had to follow a special route around the village; the first to complete the exercise was awarded a prize. So popular was the annual race that Digges had a special fund allocated for the purchase of prizes.

**Chilham Castle and Grounds**
All that is left of the castle is the keep, but this alone is impressive. Digges' splendid Jacobean home is unfortunately not open to the public. However, the keep and the spectacular grounds that were sculptured by Capability Brown are open at various times of the year for Jousting Tournaments and falconry displays.
Open: Daily from the middle of March to the middle of October. Call for specific details.
Telephone: (0) 1227 730319. Address: Chilham Village.

**St. Mary's Church**
Church records give a continuous list of vicars since 1321 but there had been a church on the site for centuries before then. The Domesday Book of 1086 tells us "...there is a church there and six mills and a half worth six pounds

and eight shillings and two fisheries worth 17 pence..."
The style of church is considered English Perpendicular and is built of flint and stone. Until 1784, it had a wonderful spire but this became unstable and had to be removed. The superb set of eight bells and clock date from 1720. The tower, standing approximately 68 feet, provides a wonderful view of the beautiful Stour Valley.

An ancient sarcophagus with a damaged cross on the lid sits in the northeast corner of the church. Some believe this coffin held the remains of St. Augustine and was moved to Chilham when Canterbury Cathedral was plundered in 1535 after Henry VIII pronounced himself head of the church.

There are some that say a hooded monk holding a flickering candle appears in the churchyard on stormy nights. He approaches a skeleton horse and they both walk backwards and disappear into the churchyard wall.

## Food for thought:
### The White Horse Pub

Tucked in the northeast corner of the square is the White Horse pub. It was once the home and vicarage of the Rev. Sampson Hieron. The reverend died in 1677 but still visits on occasions. It is said he appears mid-morning, standing in front of the inglenook fireplace, deep in thought. Those who have seen him say that his hair is gray and he is dressed in a black gown and gaiters.

The pub is considered the "favorite haunt" of the local people and is known for the fine range of ales and traditional English style food. They serve a Sunday Roast consisting of roast meat, roast potatoes, Yorkshire pudding and fresh vegetables. On a warm summer's day, the beer garden is open and is a great place to enjoy a pint of the local brew.

Telephone: (0) 1227 730355. Address: The Square, Chilham.

## If you decide to stay:
### Stour Valley House
Stour Valley House is situated between the villages of Chilham and Chartham. The guest rooms have bathrooms en suite and are non-smoking. An English breakfast is served each morning and an evening meal can be arranged upon request. The walks and views of the countryside are spectacular.
Telephone: (0) 1227 738991. Address: Pilgrims Lane, Chilham.

## Neighboring places of interest:
### Canterbury
Located about 5 miles east of Chilham is the city of Canterbury. Canterbury Cathedral is a World Heritage site and has been a place of pilgrimage since medieval times. The distance between Canterbury and London is approximately 65 miles. This was considered a day's horse ride if a certain speed was maintained. The term "canter" used to describe this speed is believed to have derived from the Canterbury-to-London journey.

### Canterbury Cathedral
In 597, the Pope sent word from Italy that St. Augustine and several other monks should travel to England to convert the ancient Britons to Christianity. King Ethelbert was the first English King to be baptized. The baptismal took place at the Saxon font in St. Martin's church. After his conversion, the king gave a large donation to St. Augustine and also bequeathed a generous amount of land to the monks' cause. With this donation, St. Augustine built

a church on the site of the cathedral; it was consecrated in 602.

The cathedral is probably best known for the murder of St. Thomas à Becket. He was a skillful and charismatic monk who was brutally slain at the hands of four knights who thought they were on a mission from King Henry II. In a heated discussion, it is believed the king said, "Who will rid me of this meddlesome priest?" The knights, who incorrectly interpreted his words as a veiled instruction to kill Becket, set off immediately for Canterbury. They arrived in Canterbury on December 29th and found St. Thomas taking refuge in the cathedral. St. Thomas clutched a pillar and, according to observations of the monk Edward Grim, who was hiding nearby, St. Thomas said, "...I am ready to die for my Lord, that in my blood the Church may obtain liberty and peace. But in the name of Almighty God, I forbid you to hurt my people whether clerk or lay." The knights, unable to drag St. Thomas outside, killed him on the spot. The last and fatal blow to his head and was so vicious the knight's sword was broken by the impact.

When the king heard of this murderous deed he was outraged. The knights who performed the act were disgraced and the king mourned the death of St. Thomas for years. It is said that several miracles happened on the site of St. Thomas' death. The king was so tortured that he traveled to Canterbury four years later and walked barefoot, dressed in a cloth sack and was flogged by monks as a penance.

During the Reformation under the direction of King Henry VIII, the remains of St. Augustine and St. Thomas à Becket were supposed to have been burned. However, there is some evidence that the monks anticipated this edict and removed the bones from their tombs and hid them elsewhere. Some believe the remains of St. Augustine were taken to Chilham for protection and housed in a sarcophagus in St. Mary's church. The fate of St. Thomas' remains is unknown.

Open: 9:00 a.m. until 6:30 p.m. daily. April through September.

9:00 a.m. until 5:00 p.m. October through March.

Canterbury Tourism Center (0) 1277 766567 Address: 34 St. Margaret's Street.

**Canterbury Heritage Museum**

An award-winning museum in an ancient house built in 1373. The building was once used as an almshouse, which were given to retired clergy or poor people of a village. An impressive feature of the home is the splendid oak roof of the Great Hall, which dates from the 14th century. The museum covers the period from the Roman invasion to the last century.

Open: Daily all year long. From 10:30 a.m. until 5:00 p.m. Monday to Saturday.

Sunday hours: 1:30 p.m. until 5:00 p.m. June until October.

Telephone: (0) 1227 452747. Address: Stour Street, Canterbury.

**Canterbury Roman Museum**

The museum houses a wonderful collection of authentic, excavated artifacts. The museum has carefully reconstructed a Roman market place, complete with a fabric seller and fruit and vegetable stalls. The reconstruction also includes a kitchen set out in authentic detail. The entrance to the Roman Museum is through two impressive pillars in Butchery Lane.

Open: Daily from 10:00 a.m. until 5:00 p.m. Monday to Saturday from June until October. Sunday: 13:30 p.m. until 5:00 p.m.
Telephone: (0) 1227 785575. Address: Butchery Lane, Canterbury.

## Walking and Hiking Information:
North Downs National Trail Office: (0) 1622 696185.
Canterbury Tales Office: (0) 1227 766567.

## Food for thought:
### The Old Weavers Tea Room
The Old Weavers Tea Room has more to offer than afternoon tea. It is a comprehensive restaurant that is open for breakfast, lunch, afternoon tea and dinner. They specialize in many of the traditional English meals such as Shepherd's Pie and lamb dishes, served with Yorkshire puddings. Savory and fruit pies are their specialty but afternoon tea is also served as part of the menu.

Telephone: (0) 1227 751343. Address: The Street, Boughton. (Approx. 6 miles from Canterbury on the Canterbury Bypass).

## How to get there:
There is regular train service from London Bridge to Chilham via Ashford.
By car: Head southeast from London on A20/M20 to Ashford. Exit at junction 9 and take A28 north towards Canterbury. Travel for about 8 miles to junction with A252 and turn left to Chilham. Chilham is approximately 60 miles away from central London.

# Biddenden

The surviving twin said, "As we came together, we will also go together." Mary and Eliza Chulkhurst were conjoined twins born in the village of Biddenden in 1100, and there they died 34 years later. On their death, they bequeathed 20 acres of land to the poor of the village and began an unusual custom that is still recognized today.

There is no grave for the Biddenden Maids in All Saints' churchyard, and little is known about the twins except their legacy. They were joined at the shoulder and hips, a rare occurrence in conjoined twins. It would have been a difficult existence for both the girls and their parents, dealing with the everyday duties and responsibilities of life. However, the family must have been financially secure because on the death of the girls, they allowed their daughters to donate 20 acres of land to the churchwardens and their successors. The acreage was used to graze cattle and raise crops, the money from which would be distributed at the discretion of the churchwardens to the poor in the village. When one of the maids died, the surviving twin appeared resolute in that her time had come as well; she lived only six hours without her beloved sister.

The ancient custom of baking "Biddenden Maids" cakes began after their death, but the actual date is unknown. In 1646 and again in 1747, molds for the cakes were found in the village. These molds show the twins' shoulders linked almost as though they are embracing each other. They are dressed in the fashion of the day with wasp-waist lines and crinoline skirts, obviously with many petticoats. On the front of one of the twins' skirts is their birth date of 1100; the other skirt has the date of their death, 1134. The depiction from the mold became the symbol that is on the village sign today.

By all accounts, the churchwardens managed the bequeathed land well and provided enough money for the ingredients necessary to bake the cakes. The original cakes were made from a simple recipe of flour and water, which must have yielded a bread-like product. They were approximately four inches long and two inches wide with an effigy of the girls imprinted on the top. The cakes and a serving of cheese were given away after the church service on Easter Monday at the discretion of the churchwardens. As word spread about the curious custom, hundreds of people visited the village at Easter time, causing such a disruption in the church that "...the conduct in the church was so reprehensible that the church wardens had to use their wands for other purposes than symbols of office..."

The ancient parish of Biddenden is believed to have contained "dens" or small forest areas where pigs or livestock could forage. Many villages and towns in England finish with the suffix "den," meaning a place in the forest. The herders used these places to fatten their livestock on acorns and beech mast before harvesting them for the winter. Each year the herders returned to the same spot in the forest with their new swineherd and this, in turn, gave them certain rights. The dens were often given the name of the families who used them, and this is believed to be the origin of "squatters' rights" in England.

## What to see and do today:
Biddenden is a small, charming village with a few shops and a little village green. The row of weavers' cottages in the High Street stands as a testament to the wealth and prosperity of the weavers during the 14th century. The cottages are home to various specialty shops, tea rooms and antique shops. The village sign depicts Mary and Eliza, the Biddenden Maids.

Today, there are no "cakes" to be distributed to the poor on Easter Monday, but some shops honor the twins by producing a biscuit (cookie) with the Biddenden Maids' impression as a special thanks to the ladies.

### All Saints' Church
It is believed there was a church on this site before the Norman Conquest in 1066, but the first recorded rector was Robert de Bradgare in 1283. The church is built of Kent sandstone with the nave, chancel and the south aisle being the original. The tower was added in the 15th century and built of Bethersden marble (local Paludina limestone with fossilized snailshells). King Edward III encouraged the trade of cloth from the area and, for this reason, the village flourished in the 14th century. There is a wonderful sculptured head believed to be Edward III and Archbishop Simon Islip in the west doorway to the south aisle.

### Biddenden Vineyard & Cider Works
Located 1.5 miles from Biddenden village, it is Kent's oldest commercial vineyard. There are 22 acres of vines, a winery and shop containing a 17th-century cider press. There are fine English wines, Kentish ciders and wonderful apple juice. Free admission and tasting.
Open: Daily with special winter hours.

Telephone: (0) 1580 291726. Address: Little Whatmans, Biddenden.

## Food for thought:
### Claris's Tea Room
A delightful place serving a wonderful choice of homemade cakes and pastries. The most famous being Claris's Cointreau cake made with a secret recipe with pure orange juice, Cointreau, and topped with a generous amount of local cream. After refreshments, browse in the shop, which specializes in offering a wide selection of local pottery.
Open: Daily 10:30 a.m. until 5:30 p.m.
Telephone: (0) 1580 291025. Address: High Street, Biddenden.

### Ye Maydes Restaurant
The Ye Maydes restaurant is a medieval building serving a fine cuisine in a friendly and cozy atmosphere. The restaurant combines French and English menus together with a fine selection of wines, making this an ideal place to visit.
Telephone: (0) 1580 291306. Address: High Street, Biddenden.

## If you decide to stay:
### Tudor Cottage
Tudor Cottage combines the character of bygone days with all the modern-day comforts and amenities. The "cat-slide roof" with attractive dormer windows and aging wooden beams make this cottage a wonderful place to stay. There are three guest rooms, all with private bathrooms. There are excellent restaurants and a traditional English pub within a few yards of the cottage.
Telephone: (0) 1580 291913. Address: 25 High Street, Biddenden.

# Neighboring places of interest:
### Tenterden
Sometimes called the "Jewel in the Weald," Tenterden became famous in the 14th century when King Edward III encouraged Flemish weavers to leave Flanders for a new start in England. In doing so, they taught the local men and women the techniques of the trade, enabling Tenterden and Biddenden to become very important villages in the cloth-making business.

The techniques used by Flemish weavers involved a process of scouring the raw wool in water, combing and stretching the cloth and treating it with fullers earth, a natural substance, to provide a smooth finish. The final stage involved pounding of the cloth, at which time it would be stretched again on wooden frames called tenters. Iron hooks were then placed along the tenters. The whole process was a long and tedious operation but the results proved so successful that many of the villagers became very wealthy and built substantial homes of quality we still see in the villages today.

The phrase "on tenterhooks" is believed to have originated with the cloth making industry, indicating that a person who is "on tenterhooks" is in great suspense or stretched to the limits of endurance.

The Tilden family of Tenterden was one of those who made their wealth from the wool industry. Nathaniel, his wife Lydia, their 7 children and 7 servants emigrated for America on the 200-ton ship *Hercules* from the port of Sandwich, Kent. They settled in Scituate, Massachusetts, and became an influential family. Samuel Jones Tilden, a descendent of Nathaniel, became a very wealthy and prominent lawyer, as well as serving as State Governor of New

York. In 1876, he ran as the Democratic candidate for President but was narrowly defeated.

**Trips by Train**
There are special day trips to surrounding towns and villages using delightful steam engines and Pullman Coaches restored to their original splendor. Some of the special events include: A day with Thomas the Tank Engine, Tenterden Folk Festival and the magical Bodiam Castle. Meals are served on the trains, varying from a continental breakfast to a six course evening meal.
Telephone: (0) 1580 765155. Address: Tenterden Town Station, Tenterden, Kent.

## Food for thought:
**Peggotty's Tea Shop**
Peggotty's Tea Shop offers a wide variety of homemade cakes and scones, and specializes in afternoon Cream Teas. It is a 17$^{th}$-century tea shoppe with all the character and charm of those bygone days. There are over 17 different cakes, pastries and scones to sample — most of them homemade.
Telephone: (0) 1580 764393. Address: 122 High Street, Tenterden.

## If you decide to stay:
**The Collina House Hotel**
The hotel is family run, using all homegrown vegetables and fruits when available. The chefs are Swiss-trained and offer a variety of meals and a wonderful dessert trolley containing between 20–30 desserts. There are 14 guest bedrooms, all with bathrooms en suite.
Telephone: (0) 1580 764852. Address: 5 East Hill, Tenterden, Kent.

### Tenterden Vineyard Park
The vineyard produces the largest quantity of sparkling wines in the area and supplies many of the shops and restaurants at home and abroad. Wine tasting, herb garden, plant center and a café are all on the premises. Lunch on the verandah is a must.
Open: Daily from 10:00 a.m. until 5:00 p.m. Saturday and Sunday: 11:00 a.m. until 5:00 p.m.

## For more information:
Tenterden Tourist Information. From April until October. Telephone: (0) 1580 763572. Address: The High Street, Tenterden.

## How to get there:
There is no direct train or bus service from London to Biddenden; however, it is possible to take a train from London Bridge to Ashford, from where Biddenden can be reached by taxi. The easiest way to get there is by car.

**By car:** Head southeast from London on A20/M20 to Maidstone. Exit at junction and take A229 south to the junction with A262. Turn left and head east on A262 to Biddenden. Biddenden is approximately 56 miles away from central London.

# Leeds Castle

The first castle on this spot was built by a Saxon lord called Ledian (Leed) during the reign of Ethelbert, King of Kent, in 857. Ledian noticed how the River Len formed a large lake with two islands in a hollow. He selected this natural defensive position to build a wooden castle complete with drawbridge. After the invasion by William the Conqueror in 1066, much of Kent was given to Bishop Odo, William's half-brother. After Bishop Odo fell out of favor with William, the castle was given to a Norman baron, Hamon de Crevecoeur who had fought alongside William during the invasion. The strategic location of the castle was not lost on de Crevecoeur who began building a stone structure in 1119. In 1287, the castle was given to King Edward 1st and Queen Eleanor of Castile.

King Henry VIII loved the castle and spent time beautifying the grounds and building new additions, such as the Maiden's Tower. Henry was a powerful man standing over 6 feet tall with auburn hair and blue eyes. He became king on April 5th, 1509 at 17 years of age. He was a practiced musician, excellent linguist and accomplished theologian. Unfortunately, he was consumed by the desire of providing a legitimate male heir to the throne of England. It is not known for sure how many of Henry's wives came to visit the castle but it is assumed that at least Catherine of Aragon and Anne Boleyn enjoyed its comforts.

The six wives of Henry made a sorrowful chapter in the history of England. He was known to be a hard and ruthless man who treated people harshly, especially some of his wives. His first marriage to Catherine of Aragon lasted over 20 years and although she produced several children, most died prematurely or were stillborn. Only one child, Mary, survived. It appears from records that although Henry had been a relatively good husband, he had several mistresses during his marriage to Catherine. He became frustrated with the lack of a male heir to the throne of England and argued with the Pope for an annulment of the marriage. The rift between Rome and the king turned into the Reformation and the establishment of the Church of England. Henry turned his attention to a young woman called Anne Boleyn, who was lady-in-waiting to the queen.

Anne Boleyn was thrilled the king favored her above the other ladies-in-waiting. Her sister Mary had been the king's mistress for some time, and it was said that she had given him an illegitimate son. Now it was Anne who caught the king's eye. She was very different from Catherine of Aragon, who had a fair complexion. By comparison, Anne had black hair and a swarthy appearance and eyes so dark, some people in court said she glared at them and used them as a weapon. Anne took full advantage of her new position and flaunted her family and friends at court, many of whom were given special privileges by the king. In an attempt to discredit Anne, some members at court said she had a sixth finger on her left hand, several ugly moles on her body and even a goiter in her neck. However, none of this appears to have bothered Anne as she dressed in an exquisite gown made of gold fabric and trimmed in fur as she traveled up the Thames to marry the waiting king. The procession began at Greenwich with hundreds of barges that were decorated with flowers and had banners streaming from the masts.

On September 7, Anne gave birth to Elizabeth, who would become a powerful and long-lived queen. After several miscarriages and stillbirths with no male heir, Anne fell out of favor with the king. A terrible plan was put in effect to accuse her of incest, adultery, and also that she had made threats on the king's life. The accusations carried a penalty of death either by fire or ax; the decision would be made at the king's discretion. Anne's own uncle the Duke of Norfolk presided over the case and gave the final verdict. The king chose the ax for a quick and merciful death and an expert executioner from France was summoned to perform the duty. Instead of traveling up the Thames to the Tower of London in all her finery as she had done 3 years earlier, Anne was probably admitted through Traitors' Gate and taken immediately to the Tower Green. The executioner was able to remove Anne's head with one blow, and the king, who was believed hunting in Epping Forest at the time, only returned to the castle when he heard the gun salute indicating the terrible deed was done.

Within a short period, the king married Jane Seymour whom he had also met at court. Jane was a quiet and demure woman and must have been concerned for her future. The king believed he had finally found the woman who could give him his sought-after son and heir. He was correct in his beliefs because Jane gave birth at Hampton Court Palace to a boy who was christened Edward on October 15th, 1537. Two weeks after the birth, Jane died of complications and a distraught king had her buried in St. George's chapel at Windsor Castle. He had been in the process of preparing a burial site for himself at St. George's chapel but the unexpected death of Jane caused him to allow her to be buried at the chapel instead. She would be the only one of Henry's six wives to be buried with the king.

The death of Jane must have affected the king greatly because he did not marry again for over two years. He may have felt that since he had a son and heir, it was unnecessary but Cromwell began searching for a new bride for Henry immediately. The importance of an allegiance with a bride from another country who supported the Reformation was a prime consideration. The Duke of Cleves had two sisters, Amelia and Anne, both of whom were readily available. A marriage between either girl would create an important alliance between the two countries. Anne was eventually chosen for Henry and she duly arrived on the shores of England. The marriage was arranged for January 6, 1540, but the king was so unhappy at her physical appearance, he referred to her as the "Flanders Mare." A letter from Anne of Cleves to the king shows her diplomacy when she suggests the relationship should be that of "brother and sister." The skill Anne showed in dealing with the delicate situation probably saved her life and the marriage ended in divorce six months later.

Catherine Howard, lady-in-waiting to Anne of Cleves, had tremendous spirit and a youthful body, which encouraged the king to take her as his 5th wife. He often called her his "rose without a thorn" but she chose the handsome, younger men of court as her lovers, causing heartache and anguish for the king. At first, the king refused to believe his beautiful wife was unfaithful even though he knew she had been promiscuous before their marriage. Catherine was sentenced to death for her adulterous behavior and was beheaded on Tower Green on February 13, 1542.

The 6th and final wife of Henry was Catherine Parr. Catherine had been twice married to older men and nursed them until their end. She was a quiet and gentle woman interested in the arts and religion and capable of calming the king's notorious temper. Towards the end of his life, he would allow only Catherine to wrap his legs that had weeping, painful ulcers. Catherine provided the king with a needed friend, nurse and companion. Mary and Elizabeth had been estranged from their father for some time but Catherine encouraged them to visit and the king was grateful to her for bringing his family together. Henry died on January 28, 1547, and Catherine was free to marry again.

As part of a history test, English children were often asked the fate of Henry's six wives. A little rhyme was devised to help them: "Divorced, beheaded, died; divorced, beheaded, survived."

## What to see and do today:
Leeds Castle is reputed to be the loveliest castle in the world. Surrounded by lakes and streams, it sits majestically in spectacular grounds that received the attention of Capability Brown in the 19th century.

Henry's Banqueting Hall is considered one of the most impressive rooms at the castle. It has a rare and unusual ebony floor with double dovetailed joints. A life-size knight on horseback commissioned by the 7th Lord Lumney for his own castle now adorns a room in Leeds castle.

In 1287, the castle was given to Edward I and his lovely wife, Eleanor of Castile. Their life together was said to be happy and rewarding and when Eleanor died of a fever as she accompanied him on one of his battles, he had her body taken to London to be buried at Westminster Abbey. As the burial procession stopped at intervals along the journey, crosses were erected in her memory. The king often referred to Eleanor as "Chere Reine" meaning "Dear Queen." The most famous of these crosses is Charing Cross, in London. To this day, a flag flies on the masthead of the gloriette portion of Leeds Castle in honor of the queens of England. The last owner of the castle was Lady Baillie whose mother was an American from the family of Witney.

**The Aviary**
The aviary at the castle tries to encourage the breeding of over 100 rare and unusual birds, with the hope of generating public interest in their preservation. Some of the birds are on the brink of extinction, and it is hoped the program will help conserve the different species and allow them to be reintroduced to the wild.

**Maze/Grotto and Gardens**
Try to find the center of the maze and stand on the mold to get a wonderful panoramic view of the castle, gardens and park. Once the center of the maze is found go underground to visit the Grotto, where tunnels are guarded by mythical beasts.

The Culpeper family owned the castle in the 17th century and set about providing a delightful, walled garden of ancient bricks. Enclosed in the garden are various rose and lavender bushes, and an herb garden that all give off a wonderful fragrance.

The Lady Baillie Garden overlooks the water and is planted with sub-tropical plants such as banana trees and other exotic shrubs that flourish in the sheltered environment in the grounds.

**The Leeds Castle Golf Course**
The nine-hole Leeds Castle Golf Course was added in 1930 for Lady Baillie and is open to the public on a fee basis, but golfers must watch out for peacocks in the grounds. Clubs can be rented at the Golf Shop that also sells golfing equipment.

Telephone: Leeds Castleline (0) 870 600 8880. Address: Leeds Castle, Maidstone.
Open: From March to October from 10:00 a.m. until 5:00 p.m. for the parks and gardens.
11:00 a.m. until 5:30 p.m. for admission to the castle.
From November to February 10:00 a.m. until 3:30 p.m. for the parks and gardens.
10:15 a.m. until 3:30 p.m. for admission to the castle.

## Food for thought:

The Fairfax Hall is a spectacular timbered barn standing in the stable yard at Leeds Castle. A plaque dates it at 1680. The owner at the time, Lord Culpeper, was head of the influential family in Kent. Culpeper's daughter married the 5th Lord Fairfax. The hall is named after their son, the 6th Lord Fairfax, who spent a large part of his life in Virginia. There he became friends with George Washington and became somewhat of a mentor to the young man. Washington's diary tells of Lord Fairfax sending him on a trip to the Blue Ridge Mountains to survey the area.

The Fairfax Hall houses a self-serve restaurant while the adjacent Terrace Room with table service provides lunches and afternoon tea.

## Neighboring places of interest:
### Aylesford
The town of Aylesford has an ancient Carmelite Friary whose founders from Mount Carmel, Palestine, settled in Kent around 1242. The original Carmelite Friary was dissolved by Henry VIII but was eventually rebuilt and is now an important pilgrimage destination.

About two miles north of Aylesford on the Weald is a Neolithic Burial chamber called "Kit's Coty House." A plaque at the site states that it is "Part of a rectangular stone burial chamber which stood at the east end of a large mound or barrow and was built during the early Neolithic era — 3500–2800 BC by Britain's early farming community. Long barrows are a rare survival of an ancient civilization and are often associated with other ritual monuments of various periods. Kit's Coty is part of a small group in Kent and perhaps the best preserved example."

Some people believe the stones have magical powers and were placed above Ley Lines. Members of the "New World Travellers" can sometimes be seen at the site dowsing and meditating. They believe Ley Lines have a magnetic force and that various important churches and meeting places are laid out on these lines. These lines can be seen easily from the air and pilots have used them to guide them in flight. Some believe that UFOs have flown along ley lines further enhancing the belief that some kind of magnetic force is present along them.

## How to get there:
There is a combined train and bus service from London to Leeds Castle. Trains leave Victoria Station about once every hour throughout the day for Bearsted Station in Kent. From Bearsted the buses operate on schedules designed to coordinate with train arrivals and departures.
**By car.** Travel southeast out of London on the M20. Exit at junction 8, about 4 miles east of Maidstone. Follow the brown-and-white tourist signs to the castle. Leeds Castle is about 25 miles from central London.

# *East Sussex*

## Burwash

Rudyard Kipling so loved the village of Burwash that he purchased the Bateman House without a second thought. He described his first sight of the home, "...we had seen an advertisement of her, and we reached her down an enlarged rabbit-hole of a lane. That's her! Make an honest woman of her — quick! We entered and felt her Spirit — her Feng Shui — to be good. We went through every room and found no shadow of ancient regrets, stifled miseries, nor any menace, though the new end of her was three hundred years old."

Called England's greatest storyteller, Rudyard Kipling was born on December 30, 1865 in Bombay, India. His father taught art in the local college and by all accounts, they lived a happy and privileged life in the English colony. Part of that advantage was to have native servants and nannies for the children. Rudyard loved his nanny and learned Hindi from her, so that he was bilingual almost from birth. It was perhaps during childhood, as he soaked up the atmosphere, the noises and smells of India together with a later feeling of abandonment that inspired him to write the *Jungle Book*.

When he was about six years old, Rudyard's parents sent him back to England to live temporarily with a family on the south coast of England. They believed this was the best they could do for their son; to live and be educated in

England. Unbeknown to them, this would be a terrible experience for the young boy who never complained but suffered terribly. It was not until he had a nervous breakdown when he was about 12 years of age that his mother learned of his suffering. She had returned to England and quickly placed him in a school in Devonshire. Whatever happened to Rudyard during those childhood years was never discussed, although the experience possibly influenced much of his work later in life.

It was noticed early in his childhood that Rudyard had extremely poor eyesight, something that would plague him for the rest of his life. Because of this, he was unable to participate in field sports such as rugby and cricket, and so took refuge in literature. His headmaster encouraged him, and it was during this time that Rudyard gave us a glimpse of his extraordinary talent to write short stories, poems and ballads.

Although Rudyard was happy in England, the need to return to India was strong and he returned when he was 17. He took a position with the Military Gazette in Lahore and worked hard — always more than 10 hours a day and often more. He provided fillers for the newspaper in the form of sketches, poems and short stories. These were collected at a later date and assembled in a book called *Plain Tales from the Hills*. The quality of his work was soon recognized and he was offered a position at *Pioneer*, a publication in Allahabad, where he wrote some of his most famous stories: *Soldiers Three*, *Wee Willie Winkie*, and many others.

When Rudyard was 25 years old, he decided to leave India and return to England via America. He traveled with Professor and Mrs. Hill, who had been friends in India and were returning to her family home in Pennsylvania. They invited Rudyard to stay with them at their home. He stayed with them for some time but returned to England in 1889 and met a young American woman called Caroline Balestier. Carrie, as Rudyard called her, was the sister of Wolcott Balestier, a dear friend and colleague who had recently died. The couple became inseparable and fell deeply in love. A friend and famous novelist, Henry James, gave Caroline away at the wedding in Chelsea, London, and the couple began their married life together.

Buoyed with success, Rudyard arranged an extravagant honeymoon around the world but he soon discovered that his savings bank had closed its doors and he would never recover his money. Facing financial ruin, the young couple surrendered the balance of their tickets and returned to Vermont where Carrie's family lived. The young couple was happy in a little home they called, Bliss Cottage, Brattleboro, Vermont. It was a cold place, especially during the winter "with snow level high with windowsill," he once wrote. It was here that he wrote his most famous books, notably *Jungle Book* and *Kim*, which are considered to be his best works. Eventually Rudyard replaced the lost money and they built a home they called Naulahka. They had two girls while they lived in America, Josephine and Elsie. The love that Rudyard felt for his children can best be seen in the two books that he wrote for them called *Just So Stories* and *Puck of Pook's Hill*.

In 1896, after a bitter quarrel with his brother-in-law, Rudyard and his little family decided to return to England. Their son John was born in a house that was owned by Rudyard's aunt Georgiana, and their life seemed idyllic until their daughter Josephine died while the family was on a trip to America in 1899. The death of his daughter must have affected Rudyard greatly but he threw himself into his work as a means of coping with his unhappiness.

Unfortunately, in 1915 his only son also died at the age of 18 at the battle of Loos.

Rudyard continued to write and raised money for the soldiers of the Boer War who returned home damaged and torn. King George V became a close and personal friend of Rudyard and the two died within three days of each other. Although he declined most of the honors bestowed on him including a knighthood, the Order of Merit and Poet Laureateship, he accepted only one, The Nobel Prize for Literature in 1907.

The love of Rudyard's work is best summed up by Somerset Maugham who said, "...our great story writer. I can't believe he will ever be equalled. I am sure he can never be excelled."

A poem about smuggling by Rudyard Kipling.
*Five and twenty ponies*
*Trotting through the dark —*
*Brandy for the parson,*
*Baccy for the clerk;*
*Laces for a lady, letters for a spy*
*And watch the wall my darling, while the Gentlemen go by!*

## What to see and do today:
The Count of Eu fought alongside William the Conqueror and was given the Manor of Burwash in 1096, as payment for his allegiance. It is a pretty village, scattered with half-timbered homes on tree-lined streets. It is easy to see why Rudyard fell in love with it and decided to make this village his permanent home.

At the end of the street stands the church of Saint Bartholomew. It is quite beautiful and was built in approximately

1090. All that remains of the Norman structure is the tower. In 1954, a rare and valuable 16$^{th}$-century German Bible was found among some old books in the vestry.

**Bateman House**
The Bateman house is located about one half mile southwest from the village and was built in 1634, probably by a wealthy ironmaster. Iron was an important commodity in the 17th century and many men found a way to capitalize on the rewards from mining the ore. It is an impressive house, originally built in the E-shaped design of many homes of that period in the area. Rudyard purchased the home in 1902 and lived there until he died in 1936. His office and study in the front window where he worked is still as it was when he died. His chair, raised by blocks to give the correct height, his oak day bed, bookcases filled to overflowing, pens and paperweights have been left just as they were when he died.

The garden and grounds around the home are particularly pretty, with the yews that Rudyard himself planted and the Maiden's Blush rosebush yielding a delicate pink rose. There is a little stream that runs through the garden giving a peaceful feeling, and a small working mill with an unique water-powered turbine that was so important to Rudyard, which still works to this day.
Telephone: (0) 1435882302. Address: Burwash, Etchingham.
Open: Daily except Thursday and Fridays from 11:00 a.m. until 5:30 p.m. Last admittance 4:30 p.m.

# Food for thought:
**The Rose and Crown**
The Rose and Crown was built in the early 17th century and is known for its good food and friendly atmosphere.

Low ceilings, exposed wooden beams and a roaring fireplace add to the delight of this pub. A varied menu is offered as well as traditional pub food. The pub also has one double and three twin rooms available for guests.
Telephone: (0) 1435 882600. Address: Ham Lane, Burwash.

## If you decide to stay:
### Glydwish Place
Glydwich Place is an out-of-the-ordinary bed and breakfast facility, located on spacious grounds with beautiful gardens and lawns. The rooms are tastefully furnished and comfortable and provide tea and coffee facilities, television and hair dryers. There is a gazebo, sauna, solarium, games room and gym available. Golf can be arranged by request.
Telephone: (0) 1435 882869. Address: Fontridge Lane, Burwash.

## How to get there:
There is no direct train service to Burwash; however, it is possible to travel from London Bridge to Etchingham, from where Burwash can be reached by taxi.
**By car**: Take A21 south out of London to Hurst Green, where you take the A265 to Burwash. Burwash is approximately 58 miles away from central London.

## Neighboring places of interest:
### Brightling
A small and sleepy village best know for the follies of Mad Jack Fuller, a Member of Parliament who was prone to building the most extraordinary structures in and around Sussex. He is entombed in the parish church at Brightling, and it is said that if a visitor runs backwards around

Fuller's pyramid tomb 7 times, you will meet up with the devil or perhaps the ghost of the eccentric Jack himself. Some of the "follies" in the area include the Brightling Needle — a 40-ft high obelisk atop the hill at Brightling, used as a beacon during the Napoleonic Wars. The Sugar Loaf, also known as Fullers Point, was given its name because of the unusual shape of the building. It was built to win a bet between Mad Jack and the vicar who said that Jack could not see the spire of Dallington Church from his house. Jack concocted the design so that he could indeed see the spire, therefore winning the wager. The Temple is a cute little house in the grounds of Brightling Park, built to resemble a Greek Temple. The Observatory sits atop the hill and has a wonderful array of instruments. Not to be left out is the Watch Tower. Mad Jack purchased Bodiam Castle in 1828 and built the tower so that he could watch the renovations in progress.

It was rumored that when Jack died, he had arranged to have his body entombed sitting in his favorite chair wearing his best top hat and with a bottle of port by his side. However, during repairs to the tomb no body was found, so it was a just prank, probably created by Mad Jack himself. He is actually buried below the church floor with an inscription that reads:
> "The boast of heraldry, the pomp of pow'r,
> And all that beauty, all that wealth e'er gave,
> Await alike th'inevitable hour.
> The paths of glory lead but to the grave."

## Food for thought:
### The Jack Fuller's Restaurant
The Jack Fuller's Restaurant was once a pub built by the man himself. Legend tells us that the local vicar wanted the pub to be located at least half a mile from the church because too many people spent their Sunday's drinking

ale instead of attending church. Mad Jack obliged the vicar in return for allowing him to build a pyramid in the churchyard where Mad Jack would eventually be buried. There are many souvenirs and information regarding the famous man at the restaurant and is considered a "must see" on the trail of the famous man.

The restaurant is known for its savory puddings, such as steak and kidney, and onion and gammon. Special attention is also paid to desserts with treacle tart and Spotted Dick, a steamed, suet pudding with currents and served with a hot custard sauce. Vegetarian dishes and salads are also a specialty.
The restaurant is closed on Monday and Tuesday.
Telephone: (0) 1424 838212. Address: High Street, Brightling.

*The Church of St. Bartholemew*

# Rye

The Lamb family was the most powerful and influential in Rye for over 150 years. James Lamb had recently been elected mayor of the town and it was only natural that when King George I was stranded on the beach of Camber Sands during a terrible storm in 1726, he would take refuge at the prestigious Lamb House. King George stayed with the family for four days using the owners' private bedroom, which they gladly surrendered for the king's use. Mrs. Lamb gave birth to a baby boy in a spare bedroom during the king's stay. They called him George in honor of the king. It's believed the king was thrilled at the event and became the boy's godfather and attended the christening.

When news came that the king and his party had been stranded on the shoreline of Camber Sands just a few miles away, James Lamb immediately went into action. His house was the most distinguished in town and he was certainly used to entertaining people of high office as part of his mayoral duties. Special meals were organized with their best china and cutlery, and the king's bed was prepared using their finest linens. The mayor knew conversation would be difficult because although the king spoke fluent French and German, he spoke very little English. Whether they used Pidgin English, sign language or interpreters, they appear to have made the best of the situation and even enjoyed it.

King George I became King of England in 1714 upon the death of Queen Anne. It is said he had little affection for England and spent hardly any time in the country. He preferred to stay in Hanover where he was most happy. He was a busy king though, overseeing Parliament and commanding the Imperial forces in the Marlborough wars. He married his first cousin, Princess Dorothea of Zell, but the marriage was an unhappy one because George was reputed to be a philanderer. The arrangement suited him until his wife became enamored with a count at court. The count mysteriously disappeared and Dorothea was sent to the castle of Ahlde where she died in 1726.

The Lamb family played a significant part in the history of Rye. James Lamb was elected Mayor thirteen times and his son continued the tradition, serving twenty terms in the same capacity. The family continued to reside at Lamb House during this time but it was sold during the 1860s.

Henry James, the famous novelist, visited Rye at a particularly low time in his career and fell in love with the town. He favored it best in the evening as the setting sun changed the natural colors of brown to deep reds and purples.

James' friends believed he retreated to Rye to escape the criticism he found in London. He was unable to accept negative comments about his works, and when his play *Guy Domville* was jeered and heckled off stage, he was mortified. Another blow came when his novel *The Europeans* was given back to him unread by G.H. Lewes. These two incidents affected him greatly, and he left London to find solace on the south coast of England.

When James arrived in Rye in 1895, he stayed at the old Vicarage and began looking for a suitable house as a permanent home. He continued to visit London for business reasons but returned immediately to his beloved Rye. In 1897, he wrote the *Spoils of Poynton* and appeared to love his life in the busy seaside town.

When Lamb House became available for lease in 1897, he jumped at the chance to live in the elegant home. He immediately fell in love with it and, according to the National Trust Guide, later said, "All the good things that I hoped of the place have in fact properly blossomed and flourished, the quiet essential amiability of Lamb House only deepens with experience." When the home was offered for sale in 1899, he purchased it for 2,000 pounds sterling. His most favored place was the walled garden in the rear of the house. He loved the flowers, birds and the insects they brought but he was not particularly interested in its upkeep and left this in the hands of a trusted gardener.

Many of James' most famous works were written at Lamb House. *The Awkward Age* was the first, followed by *The Wings of the Dove* in 1902. *The Ambassadors* was written in 1903 and *The Golden Bowl* in 1904. James moved around the house as he worked. During the winter months, he wrote in the green room on the first floor. In spring and summer, he wrote in the pavilion, which was close to the house. Unfortunately the pavilion did not survive and was lost to a bomb during World War II.

Unlike Charles Dickens and many other notable authors, James was not a good storyteller and so did not convey his work very well. His close friends Joseph Conrad and Edith Wharton were kind and attentive to him despite his lack of special oration capabilities. Edith credits much of her success to James' guidance and help because she was greatly influenced by him, especially when she wrote *The Age of Innocence*, which brought her fame and wealth.

During the 18 years that James owned the Lamb House, he entertained many notable visitors including H.G. Wells and Rudyard Kipling. Shortly before James death in 1916, H.G. Wells, who owned Lamb House, launched a bitter tirade on James' life's work. It is not known why Wells took such an action but it must have been a severe blow to a sensitive man like Henry James.

After James' death, Lamb House was on the market again and this time became the home to another writer, E.F. Benson. Benson was a satirical author known for his stories about *Miss Map, Mapp and Lucia* as well as many others. After Benson's occupation of the home, Rumer Godden, author of *The Greengage Summer* and *Black Narcissus,* also made Lamb House her home.

While Benson was living at Lamb House, another American writer, Conrad Aiken, moved to Rye in 1924. Aiken, a Pulitzer Prize winner, purchased the former Quaker meeting house in Mermaid Street, called Jeake's House, and also settled down to a quiet life in the seaside resort. Jeake's House was smaller and a little younger than Lamb House yet had all the character and charm including the sloping floors and low-beamed rooms. Aiken lived in Jeake's House for over 23 years and, like other authors living in Rye, entertained many of his friends, most notably T.S. Eliot.

## What to see and do today:
Rye is an ancient town full of charm and character. It became part of the Federation of Cinque Ports in the 13th century and provided ships to enhance the monarch's fleet. The town was often a target of the French, who plundered and burned the town.

When Queen Elizabeth I visited Rye in 1573, she was so taken with the liveliness of the town, the commerce and deportment of the people and their reception of her that she gave permission for the town to be called Rye Royal.

Nowadays, the town is famous for its inns, shops and houses that appear to almost topple into the cobbled streets below. The town has not changed much since medieval times. The wonderful quay with its fishing boats and antique shops provide a wonderful day of adventure and the beaches at Camber Sands are considered some of the finest on the south coast.

## Lamb House

James fled from London after bitter criticism of his work and took refuge in the comforting rooms at Lamb House that still display many of his personal affects. The delightful brick house and beautiful, walled garden that so captivated James and inspired him to write many of his most famous works can still be seen and enjoyed today.
Open: Wednesdays and Saturdays only from 2:00 p.m. until 6:00 p.m. April through October.
Telephone: (0) 1892 890651. Address: West Street, Rye.

## St. Mary's Church

This 900-year-old church is dedicated to St. Mary the Virgin. It has dominated the hillside in Rye and has been victim to many raids by the French. They came in 1377 and looted the town, burned the church and took off with its bells. The following year, the men of Rye and Winchelsea raided a town in Normandy and treated their town in a similar fashion, but brought the bells of St. Mary back and installed them where they belonged. The church has several beautiful stained-glass windows and an unusual clock that is considered the oldest turret clock in the England. It houses an eighteen-foot-long pendulum that was added after it was built in 1561–62 and is still in good working order.

The church and clock tower are open daily so that visitors can see the clock mechanism, the bells and the beautiful countryside around Rye.

**Rye Castle Museum**

There are two museums in the town. The first is the Ypres Tower, which is a fascinating building that has been a fort, house, jail and mortuary. It is an extraordinary building that overlooks Romney March and Rye Bay. The second museum is on East Street and contains a wide display of military uniforms, tools and pottery.

Open: Ypres Tower — April 1 to October 31, Monday, Thursday and Friday from 10:30 a.m. until 1:00 p.m./ 2:00 p.m. until 5:00 p.m.

Saturday and Sunday from 10:30 a.m. until 5:00 p.m. (both buildings)

East Street Museum -- 2:00 p.m. until 5 p.m.

Both locations closed on Tuesdays and Wednesdays.

Call for specific information: (0) 1797 226 728 or (0) 1797 223345.

*Ypres Tower*

# Food for thought:
## Swan Cottage Tea Rooms
Swan Cottage was built in 1420 as a coaching inn. It now houses a delightful tearoom that serve fresh-brewed morning coffee and toasted tea cakes. The lunch menu consists of quiches, jacket potatoes topped with various cheeses, and toasted sandwiches. Their specialty is a Welsh Rarebit, treacle and sticky puddings. Afternoon teas are served with small sandwiches, cakes and scones. The inn is reputed to be haunted by a "lady in blue" who comes out in the evening, although very few people have been lucky enough to see her.
Telephone: (0) 1797 222423. Address: 41, The Mint, Rye.

# If you decide to stay:
## The Mermaid Inn
The Mermaid Inn was founded in the 11th century and is Rye's largest medieval buildings. In the 1750s it was the headquarters of the notorious smugglers called the Hawkhurst Gang. They were known and feared by everyone, even the Customs Men who were often on their trail. The gang would sit in the Mermaid Inn with loaded pistols on the table in a threatening manner that few would challenge. When the Customs Men arrived on the scene, the gang would leave the Mermaid via a tunnel that reputedly ended up at the Old Bell Inn. The Old Bell Inn used to have a revolving door disguised as a cupboard that opened directly to the street for quick getaway. These inns provided a refuge and haven for the smugglers, whose lucrative trade was shared by many people in the town.

The Mermaid Inn today offers wonderful food and accommodation. It has retained all of its character and charm with beamed walls, ceilings, leaded windows and inglenook fireplaces. Guest rooms have bathrooms en suite,

and many are equipped with four-poster beds. In 1973, the distinctive honor of the Queen's Award to Industry for Export Achievements was given to the Mermaid Inn. This is a prized and distinctive honor greatly treasured by the owners of the inn.
Telephone: (0) 1797 223065. Address: Mermaid Street, Rye.

### The Vicarage
The Old Vicarage was awarded The Best Breakfast in England Award in 1999/2000. The guest rooms are beautifully decorated with fine fabrics and many splendid pieces of period furniture. Original parts of the house are over 400 years old, and yet modern facilities have not harmed the character of the home. Freshly baked bread, homemade jam and yogurt are just a few of the special items on the menu, as well as Romney Marsh mushrooms and homegrown tomatoes.
Telephone: (0) 1797 222119. Address: 66 Church Square, Rye.

## How to get there:
There is regular train service from London Bridge via Hastings and Ashford to Rye.

**By car**: Head southeast from London on A20 to M25. Take M25 south to junction 5. Exit onto A21 and continue about 28 miles to Flimwell. Exit onto A268 to Rye. Rye is approximately 65 miles away from central London.

# Winchelsea

The locals call it Deadman's Lane but visitors know it as Hogtrough Lane. The people who died at the site will always be remembered because the incident was etched in memories for centuries. In 1359, a contingent of 3,000 French soldiers descended on the small town intent on ransacking, butchering and looting. The town was deserted, however, and the soldiers hunted until they found the townspeople. They had taken refuge in St. Giles' church, believing they would be safe from harm in the sanctuary, but the soldiers found them and killed them where they hid. They were buried in the churchyard of St. Giles and the lane was forever known as Deadman's Lane.

The men of Winchelsea and Rye never forgot or forgave the French attack on their church and its people. Some 20 years later, they sailed to Normandy and burned and looted a town in retaliation for the day and night of terror inflicted upon their town.

There are some that believe the name of Deadman's Lane was given many years earlier when victims of the plague were buried around St. Giles' church. During the summer of 1348, the plague, or Black Death, appeared on the shores of England. The ports were the first to be infected by the rats and the fleas that carried the deadly disease in the cargoes of ships as they traveled along the old trade routes from India and the Middle East. The plague spread quickly along the coastline and up the Thames Valley into London until almost every town was infected. There were two forms of the disease; those who spat blood died within three days, the others within five. No one knew how the plague spread, with some calling it the Seeds of Doom, as it attacked everyone regardless of stature.

The country was in panic. The Black Death had taken a country of 5–6 million people and reduced it to less than 3 million. No one was immune from the disease, from royalty to peasant. King Edward's young daughter Joan succumbed, as did the Archbishop of Canterbury. Within the square mile of London, approximately 300 people died each day. Their bodies were collected in carts during the evening by men who patrolled the streets calling, "Bring out your dead." The bodies were deposited outside the walls of London in massive graves, sometimes 50,000 at a time.

A recent article in the Daily Mail reports a Rochester monk who describes the disease: "The plague carried off so vast a multitude of people of both sexes that nobody could be found who would bear the corpses to the grave. Parents carried their own children on their shoulders to the church and threw them into a common pit. From these pits such an appalling stench was given off that scarcely anyone dared even walk beside the cemeteries." The clergy who administered the sick became ill themselves and this, in turn, caused a shortage of priests throughout the country. In the same article, the Daily Mail quotes the Bishop of Bath and Wells who tells the people they could make their last confessions to a layman, or "to a woman if no man is available."

The Black Death stayed with the people of England for almost five years, and there were further sporadic outbreaks until another deadly episode in 1665. The nursery rhyme *Ring a Ring of Roses* is a direct outcome of the disease, as it fully describes the symptoms from beginning to end. An interesting difference between the English and American version is the end of the rhyme: English, all fall dead, and American, all fall down.

It is not known for sure when the Confederation of the Cinque Ports was established, but some think it began as early as Edward the Confessor's reign in 1042–66. The purpose of the confederation was to enhance the reigning monarch's arsenal by providing a fleet of fully manned ships to protect the country's southern shores, mainly from the French and others intent on piracy. In return for a commitment of a certain number of vessels for a specific number of weeks each year, the ports were given special financial privileges. King John realized the strength of the confederation and used them while he rebuilt his own fleet. He showered the original five ports of Romney, Hythe, Sandwich, Dover and Hastings with privileges almost equal to that of his barons because he knew the importance of the confederation and appreciated their value to him.

As the confederation grew, Winchelsea and Rye joined the formidable fleet, and by all accounts the seas around England were well protected for many years by highly skilled sailors. In 1294, Edward I called into service hundreds of seamen and the confederation provided 50 well-maintained, fully manned ships. Of those 50 ships, Winchelsea supplied 13, a large and impressive group that was well appreciated by the confederation.

King Edward I had taken a personal interest in the town of Winchelsea as far back as 1282 when he received a petition from the townsfolk asking for help to save their town from erosion. The king sent a commission comprised of his Treasurer and the Mayor of London, who advised the king on their return that something must to be done to help the town or the sea would consume it. No help came and then a terrible storm hit in 1287, swamping the town and diverting the River Rother. The strong winds and currents had been eating away the shoreline for years and, when the storm came, the final damage was done. The king was approached again and this time he proposed the town be moved to another location altogether and personally took an interest in the planning of the streets, wharves, cellars and administrative buildings. The site that was chosen for the New Winchelsea was on a peninsular believed to have once had the Roman village of Iham on its western boundary.

It is said that the town of Winchelsea closely resembles the town of Monsegur in southwest France, and that the king modeled Winchelsea after its likeness. The streets were designed to cross at right angles, more or less, and the merchants were situated towards the northern edge of the peninsular. Some of these merchants specialized in the import of wine (as did the king) and so it's believed the king helped design some of the houses to have deep foundations to accommodate wine cellars. Some were quite large; 30 feet long and 15 feet wide in places. Many were vaulted, built of local stone and then dressed in Caen stone. Their cellars kept the wine at a perfect temperature, and some still do to this day.

The Foissart Chronicles that were written between 1369–73 state that "Edward I was a brave, wise and resourceful ruler, enterprising and very successful in war." He traveled to the Holy Land and participated in the crusades, but he also took an interest in matters of state and the well being of his subjects, especially the little town of Winchelsea.

## What to see and do today:
The view from Winchelsea can be quite spectacular. On a clear day, the downs of Boulogne can be seen and sometimes at night the lights from Cap Griz Nez to Etaples sparkle like tiny stars in the distance.

The town sits atop a hill about two miles southwest of Rye, and still has the remains of three gates called The Strand, Pipewell or Land Gate and the New Gate. Despite its name, the New Gate was built in the 13th century and is believed to have been the gate through which the French gained access to the town in 1380. The medieval town sits as it has for centuries, with its wonderful half-timbered homes and streets arranged around St. Thomas' church. St. Giles' church no longer exists; the stone was removed and sold to help build the new harbor at Rye in 1777.

As the need for the federation diminished, the town fell into despair, although when Queen Elizabeth I visited Winchelsea in 1573, she was impressed with the town. Later, however, other travelers such as Sir Walter Raleigh (in 1601) and John Wesley in (1790) state that the town had gone into decay. The area became known for smuggling and gangs that patrolled the coastline and frequented the inns and taverns.

During the 19th century, the town began a revival of sorts and was recognized for its important historic value. Painters such as Turner and Millais found interest in the countryside and buildings. Thackeray, Coventry Patmore and Conrad as well as many other artists found the town pleasing to use as a base.

The areas of Rye and Winchelsea serve as the background for Thackeray's unfinished romantic novel *Denis Duval* that mentions Strand Gate in Winchelsea and also gives valuable insight into the town's life during the 18th century. John Millais used the background below the Strand Gate for his painting *The Blind Girl*. It is a beautiful painting, showing a young woman holding another on her lap, which also holds several books. A double rainbow can be seen in the background against a dark, brooding sky and there are horses, cattle and crows in the fields. Butterflies flit around the meadow and the artist has captured a butterfly as it settles on the girl's shawl.

**St. Thomas' Church**
The church of St. Thomas has a rather plain exterior but the interior is quite beautiful. The medieval Alard tombs and spectacular stained-glass windows that were added in the 20th century are best seen on a sunny day to fully appreciate their beauty. It's believed the center of the church was built in the 13th century, but during the 14th century the French invaded the town and scarred the church such that we can still see the damage today. Robert de Winchelsea was born in the old town in approximately 1230. He became the Archbishop of Canterbury and presided over the marriage of Edward I to Margaret, daughter of Philip III, King of France.

**The Court Hall Museum**
The displays in the museum illustrate the history of the ancient town of Winchelsea, its importance as one of the leaders of the Confederation, and the personal interest that King Edward I took in the development and planning of the town in 1287. The exhibits show a wide range of items including maps, models, pictures, pottery and the local seal. The seal dates from the early reign of Edward I (1272–1307) and shows an ancient ship with a poop and embattled forecastle, and the royal arms that consists of three lions passant. The legend reads: The seal of the Barons of our Lord the King of England of Winchelsea.

Open: 10:00 until 12:30 p.m. weekdays May to October. 2:00 p.m. until 5:00 p.m. on weekends in April. Call for specific opening times.
Telephone: (0) 1797 224395. Address: Court Hall, Winchelsea.

## Interesting walks:

### Springs Steps
There are six open wells in Winchelsea from which the citizens used to take their water. The Spring Steps leads to Queen Elizabeth's Well, and is reached along the narrow path and down some steps, which lead to the road at the bottom of the cliff. The five remaining wells are located within a few hundred yards of each other and are called Pipe Well, Friars Well, St. Katherine's Well, New Well and Vale or St.Leonard's Well. It is rumored that once an individual has sampled the water from St. Leonard's Well, his heart will remain in Winchelsea.

## The medieval gates:
### The Strand
The Strand gate is one of the original gates of the town and was built in the 13th century. The walls of the gate disappeared centuries ago although the portcullis groves can still be seen. The gate is mentioned in Thackeray's unfinished romantic novel *Denis Duval,* and Millais used the view of the town close by the gate for his painting *The Blind Girl.*

### The New Gate
The New Gate and Town Ditch are on the outskirts of town. Trees and grass now camouflage the 13th-century gate but it still gives an idea of its original splendor. It is said the French passed through this gate when they invaded Winchelsea in 1380.

### The Pipewell or Land Gate
The Pipewell Gate was destroyed during 1380 when the French invaded, but John Helde, the Mayor, rebuilt it in 1404. Not far from the gate, the cliff plummets and it was at this point that King Edward I narrowly escaped losing his life. The king had been in Winchelsea inspecting his fleet and, as he approached the top of the cliff, his horse shied from a nearby windmill and jumped a low earth wall. King and horse disappeared from sight as the villagers ran to the wall fearing the worse. They were amazed to see the horse land almost 30 feet below where it slid about 12 paces before both horse and rider came to a standstill. In the official town guide of Winchelsea, it is stated that the king remained in his saddle during the whole incident and that he "turned him around with the rein and rode him straight up to the gate. When he passed through the gate the people standing round were filled with great joy and wonder in contemplation of the divine miracle by which the King was preserved."

## Food for thought:
### The Tea Tree
The Tea Tree won an award recently from the Tea Council because of the way they prepare and serve tea in the shop. They also grind and blend their own coffee in one of the two cellars beneath the shop. The Tea Tree is housed in a 15th-century coaching inn and serves homecooked, traditional meals either in the restaurant or the courtyard garden. Vegetarian meals are available on request. The restaurant specializes in afternoon cream teas, with sandwiches, scones and small cakes. The specialties of the house are their giant meringues served, if desired, with fruit and cream.
Telephone: (0) 1797 226102. Address: 12 High Street, Winchelsea.

## If you decide to stay:
### The Strand House
The Strand is a 15$^{th}$-century listed building that was once the town's workhouse. It was built on the original town quay and overlooks National Trust farmland. The guesthouse offers a warm and hospitable atmosphere with its oak-beamed ceiling, walls and inglenook fireplace. There are ten guest bedrooms available, some with four-poster beds, and each one has its own individual charm. A traditional English breakfast using produce from the area is served each morning. There is a large garden to be enjoyed in the summer, as well as a fully licensed bar and dining room.
Telephone: (0) 1797 226276. Address: Tanyard's Lane, Winchelsea.

## How to get there:
There is indirect train service from London Victoria and Charing Cross via Ashford. Travel time is approximately 2 hours.
**By car**: Take A21 south out of London to Flimwell, and then A268 to Rye. From Rye turn west on A259 to Winchelsea. Winchelsea is approximately 70 miles away from central London.

# Bodiam

Castle Bodiam rises majestically out of the moat like the legendary sword Excalibur. It is a romantic, magical castle that inspires fairy tale images of knights, princesses and sorcerers. The Domesday Book notes a Saxon hall on the site but Sir Edward Dalyngrigge built the present structure 500 years ago. Construction started in 1385 and was completed in 1390. King Richard II granted Dalyngrigge a license to improve his manor house to "strengthen and crenellate... and make thereof a castle in defense of the adjacent countryside and for resistance against our enemies." Instead of fortifying his manor house against a possible invasion by the French, Dalyngrigge decided to build a castle suitable for a man of his station in life.

Dalyngrigge was a military man who had fought in the Hundred Years War that began in the 1300s and continued until 1451. The French had suffered disastrous defeats at the Battle of Crècy in 1346 and then again in Pointiers in 1356 when Prince Edward, otherwise known as the Black Prince, captured Prince John of France and asked for a ransom of 3 million crowns. The ransom was paid and Prince John was returned unharmed to his people.

Dalyngrigge returned to England in approximately 1380 with his new wife, intent on providing a loving and safe environment for his family. There were constant threats from the French in retaliation for the defeats they had suffered, so Dalyngrigge decided to improve his manor house and fortify it in readiness for an attack. He was already a wealthy man from an influential family in Sussex, but now his coffers were overflowing from the fortune he had brought back from France. He reconsidered the plan to reinforce his present manor house and decided to build a castle instead.

The overall design of the castle is unusual in that it is set in a rectangular, lake-like moat that is fed by the river Rother. Previously, there had been a bridge that turned at right angles to the octagonal stone-case island. The purpose of the right angle turn was to expose the right, unshielded, flank of any besieging force to the castle's defenders. It would have been a formidable castle to capture because when a castle was under siege, one of the most common means of entry was tunneling. An invading army would travel underground until they reached an outer wall and cause it to collapse. Sometimes they would set a fire at the end of the tunnel to cause even more damage.

The owners of Bodiam castle were only called upon to defend themselves twice in 600 years, and then from their own countrymen. On both occasions it was surrendered relatively easily. In 1483, it was briefly captured by the errant Sir Thomas Lewknor and taken from him by the Earl of Surrey for his king, Richard III. The second occasion was during the English Civil War when Roundhead soldiers (Parliamentary) under the guidance of Oliver Cromwell directed that all the kingdom's castles should be "slighted." The soldiers almost completely gutted the internal structure but the exterior was not as easy to destroy and they had to leave the walls virtually intact.

Although the French did attack Rye and Winchelsea as well as many other towns along the coast, they never made an assault on Bodiam castle.

In 1828, "Mad Jack Fuller," an eccentric Member of Parliament, purchased the castle. He is known for building several unusual structures, like the Watch Tower that he built so that he could watch the renovations on Bodiam castle from a distance. He was a large and extremely loud individual who demanded attention. Even in death he caused disruption by being entombed in a pyramid structure in the churchyard at Brightling. Rumor had it that he was buried in his best clothes with his finest top hat and a plate of chicken and a bottle of port at his side but during repairs recently, this was proven not to be true. Folklore tells us that if a visitor runs backwards around Fuller's pyramid tomb 7 times, you will meet up with the devil or perhaps the ghost of the eccentric Jack himself.

The last owner of Bodiam Castle was Lord Curzon, who was once the Viceroy of India. He purchased it in 1917 and began an extensive restoration program that continued until he died in 1925. It was then bequeathed to the National Trust, who continued the work and carefully maintained the castle that is considered second only to Leeds in its beauty.

The village of Bodiam and the surrounding hop gardens were a haven for migrant workers and travelers. During medieval times, many inns sprang up to accommodate travelers on pilgrimages, knights on missions and clergymen. Since most people did not read or write, a sign would be hung on the outside of the inn to indicate to travelers that it was a place of rest and replenishment. Sometimes the sign would signify an allegiance towards the church or the Crown with names such The Monk's Habit or The

Royal Oak. These signs were the forerunners of pub signs today, and many of them have retained their original names for centuries.

Beer was an important drink during these times, not only as a pleasurable beverage but also sometimes as a necessity because fresh water was not always available. The abundance of hop gardens and inns producing beer brought the dreaded Inspector of Ales who was appointed by the manorial authorities to monitor the sale of beer. During medieval times, it was customary to wrap a garland of ivy on tall poles outside the inn to indicate a new batch of ale was ready to sell. The inspector's appearance at an inn could be of great concern to a landlord because he could ruin the landlord's reputation and even cause him grievous bodily harm.

The inspector, or Ale-Conner as he was often called, traveled from village to village searching for inns that had produced a new batch of ale. He would appear unexpectedly, dressed in leather breeches and ask for a jug of beer. After pouring some beer on a wooden bench, he would squat in the puddle he had made. He would then converse with all those around him, accepting their offers of beer and good company but never once moving or changing his position in any way. After about thirty minutes he would rise from the wooden bench. If his leather breeches stuck to the bench, this meant the beer had not been properly fermented; if he could rise easily from his seat, the batch was good. The penalty for selling beer that had not been properly fermented or knowingly giving short measures of beer was often an hour in the village stocks, where the innkeeper was bombarded with rotten fruit and eggs.

## What to see and do today:

The River Medway runs close to the small village of Bodiam and is surrounded by lush green fields where sheep and cows graze. During Roman times, the village of Bodiam was an important location because of its easy access to Battle and the other towns of Sedlescombe, Staplecross and Stonegate. These towns and villages were rich in iron, an important commodity that enabled many people to become wealthy. Once the iron had been mined, it was made into ingots that were shipped all over England and also to mainland Europe.

### Bodiam Castle

Bodiam was one of the last medieval castles to be built in England, at a time when feudal retainers were no longer used to defend a castle and its owner. Instead, mercenaries were used, having an affect on the castle design. The garrison was separated through elaborate measures from Sir Edward and his family to ensure that in case of a mutiny Sir Edward would retain control of key strategic resources such as the water supply and the strongest of the curtain towers.

It seems almost impregnable with its deep moat and appears to glisten in the sunlight. The castle is absolutely breathtaking and conjures up images of chivalrous knights galloping across the bridge towards the main gate. Although the interior is still in ruins, the castle still shows perfectly what a real castle was like with its double gatehouse and towers, portcullis, narrow windows and arrow slits. There are special features during the year of medieval pageants and other related activities.

The National Trust has a tea room on site that offers morning coffee, a light lunch or afternoon tea.

*Bodiam Castle*

Open: Daily from 10:00 a.m. until dusk from mid-February until October 31. November to February open on Saturday and Sunday from 10:00 a.m. until 4:00 p.m. Call for details.
Telephone: (0) 1580 830436. Address: Bodiam.

**Kent and East Sussex Railway**
The railway runs approximately 11 miles through some of the prettiest scenery in the country. The beautifully restored railway and coaches comprise of working engines from America, Norway and, of course, England. Passengers can enjoy a delicious meal on a living and moving museum and see the sights as they travel behind a restored steam engine. Special features include: A Day Out With Thomas the Tank; Tenterden Folk Festival; Austin Counties Car Rally, and many others. The train links to Tenterden, Northiam and Bodiam Castles. Telephone for special events and details.
Telephone: (0) 1580 765155. Address: Tenterden Town Station.

## Food for thought:
### The Castle Inn
The Castle Inn is located directly across the road from the parking lot at Bodiam Castle. It was rebuilt in 1885 and has retained all the wooden beams, roaring fireplace and atmosphere from centuries passed. It is also reputed to have a ghost of a child although the staff has never been lucky enough to see him. The inn was the first pub to be opened by the famous brewer, Guinness, and offers a wonderfully terraced beer garden where a pint may be enjoyed. There are a variety of meals including an excellent Sunday roast dinner and an à la Carte meal offered each evening. Vegetarian and special meals for children are prepared on request.

Telephone: (0) 1580 830330. Address: High Street, Bodiam.

## If you decide to stay:
### Elms Farm
The Elms bed and breakfast is actually a full working farm and livery yard. There is a 17th-century barn on site and an oast house with a roundel where the hops used to be dried. A full English breakfast is served each morning, and there are two good restaurants for an evening meal within a few minutes walk in either direction.

Telephone: (0) 1580 830494. Address: Bodiam, Robertsbridge.

## How to get there:
There is no direct train service to Bodiam; however, it is possible to travel from London Bridge to Etchingham, from which Bodiam can be reached by taxi.

**By car:** Take A21 south out of London to Flimwell, where you take the A268 to Hawkhurst. In Hawkhurst take the A229 south. After about a mile take the left fork (B2244).

After about 2 miles, look for signs on your left to Bodiam. Bodiam is approximately 52 miles away from central London.

## Neighboring places of interest:
### Great Dixter and Gardens
The splendid home is an excellent example of a 15th-century half-timbered manor with a unique combination of tic-and-hammer beams that is rarely seen. It was enlarged by Sir Edwin Lutyens and has been completely restored to its former beauty. During the renovations, domestic accommodations were added, as was another wing comprised of a hall house from around the-mid 1500s. The hall was originally built in Beneden and fell on hard times but it was rescued, carefully dismantled and rebuilt at Gr. Dixter. The house is quite beautiful and is not only an historic house but also the family home of Christopher Lloyd.

The exquisite gardens are an extension of the love and care that is seen in the home. The garden is a haven filled with color, diversity and texture. It is the mastermind of Christopher Lloyd and his chief gardener, Fergus Garrett. They created ponds and a formal pool with beautiful and unusual plants. The borders around the gardens are exceptionally pretty and show tremendous attention to detail so that there are flowers in bloom for most of the year. There is a nursery and gift shop at Gr. Dixter, where many of the seeds and plants that are seen in the gardens can be purchased. A catalog is available giving a description of these plants and bulbs.
Open: Tuesday through Sunday from 2:00 p.m. until 5:00 p.m. from April to October.
Telephone: (0) 1797 252878. Address: Dixter Road, Northiam.

# **Battle**

On October 14, 1066, life in England changed forever. The Britons, accustomed as they were to invasions from Vikings as well as internal rivalry between its earls, now faced their most formidable opponent. The Duke of Normandy, otherwise known as William the Bastard, had amassed an army to invade England and take its crown as his own. William believed the sovereignty had been unjustly taken from him after his distant cousin, Edward the Confessor, had died. King Harold, his two brothers, Leofwine and Gyrth, their castle guards and thousands of knights and foot soldiers met the duke on Senlac ridge. Harold's men were tired. They had marched 195 miles north to fight King Hardrada of Norway at Stamford Bridge and then turned southward and fast marched 250 miles to defend their beloved king and country.

King Edward the Confessor was dying and had left no heir. The Witan, a group of wise men whose primary duty was to advise the king, met to decide who should be his successor. There were several candidates, including the Duke of Normandy who was related by marriage. He had a legitimate claim but he was a foreigner and the Witan felt they needed to look closer to home for the future king. They believed their prayers were answered when the dying king took Harold's hand and said, "…I also commend to you those men who have left their native land for love of me and served me faithfully. Take an oath of fealty from them if they wish, and protect and retain them..." With these words, the Witan believed the king had voiced his wishes that Harold should succeed him and they planned the coronation of the new king.

A military man, Harold was over 40 years of age and his devotion to the king was well known. He was not of royal blood but his military prowess, proven so often on the battlefield, was legendary. He was crowned King of England at Westminster Abbey on January 6, 1066, but it would be a short-lived reign. His style of commanding men was very different from his predecessor, who had never traveled far from home and was out of touch with his armies. When Harold heard that people living in Northumbria did not accept his sovereignty, he took a small party of men and traveled north to meet with them and gain their loyalty. The earls of Northumbria were amazed by the king's visit and pledged their fealty, which would be desperately needed in the months to come.

According to the Anglo-Saxon Chronicles, a "long haired star" appeared in the sky on April 24, and shone there for 7 nights. This was seen as an ill omen by the king's astrologers but if Harold was disturbed by it, he did not show his concern and simply continued with the duties of state.

It was not long before news came that William, Duke of Normandy, was building ships and amassing an army. The ominous threat of an invasion had been rumored for months but now the king's sources told him an attack was imminent.

The battle at Stamford Bridge on September 25, 1066 against the king of Norway was victorious for the British army but they had little time to celebrate, as news came that William intended to land at Pevensey. Harold had marched his army 195 miles north in five days to battle the Norwegian king and now the threat came from the south coast of England. He immediately turned his army around and fast marched southward to Pevensey, a distance of 250 miles. The trek was accomplished in 13 days, an unbelievable military maneuver for those times.

William landed on the coastline of Pevensey and marched approximately 6 miles inland. Waiting to meet him, Harold and his men took the advantage on Senlac ridge a natural, defensive position. As day broke on October 14, the two armies faced each other. The English had a distinct advantage with 11,000 troops against possibly only 8,000 Norman soldiers. The Norman army used their expert archers to fill the sky with waves of arrows that pierced the English troops' armor and they dropped in the hundreds. Still, the English were able to advance and counterattack. If Harold had taken a more disciplined and strategic approach at this point, he may well have won the battle. Instead, his weary men chased a group of Norman knights and by doing so, left their posts unguarded. William, seeing this tactical advantage, gave signals to his knights to appear as though they were retreating. The English soldiers once again took off after the Norman knights leaving their positions undefended. It was not long before both flanks of the English army were in complete disarray and vulnerable to attacks from the rear.

Some have said that Harold's life was taken by a small band of Norman knights who stormed the defensive lines and hacked Harold to death, but the most common belief is that he died from an arrow in the eye. Perhaps both stories are correct because his body was so badly mutilated that his wife Edith had to identify him by personal marks on his body.

The famous Bayeux tapestry fully describes the battle on Senlac ridge and its aftermath. The tapestry was most likely inspired and commissioned by Bishop Odo, William's half-brother, in 1070. The bishop was given a good part of Kent as a reward for his services, but he was a cruel and ambitious man who soon fell out of favor with William. The type of stitches and colors of yarn that were used indicates the local women of Kent probably made the tapestry. There are over 70 scenes of shipbuilding, farming and other everyday activities providing a valuable, detailed account of everyday life during those times. The tapestry was badly treated for hundreds of years but it was finally given to the Bishop of Bayeux in 1792. It now hangs in the museum at Centre Guillaume le Conquerant, Rue de Nesmond, Bayeux, France. The tapestry holds a wealth of information from the depiction of the death of Edward, from his wife cradling his feet in her lap to Harold trying desperately to pull an arrow from his eye. The tapestry also provides an insight into the battle itself, the lives of the people, their trades and how they earned their living.

William the Conqueror was crowned King of England on Christmas Day 1066. In 1086, he sent his scribes throughout England to document every village and town, every inhabitant, their homes, barns, livestock against which a tax could be levied. This information was compiled into a large book. The people of England were so afraid of this development they called it the Domesday Book after God's final Day of Judgment. The Domesday Book measured land by "hundreds," meaning a parcel was large enough to support 100 families. Each family unit was called a "hide," but the actual size was vague and varied from county to county. For instance, a hide in Sussex was about 40 acres and in East Anglia it was about 120 acres.

*Abbey Ruins*

## What to see and do today:
The town is a bustling, busy place with a 14th-century majestic gatehouse at the entrance to the town. It is still intact and almost appears to be a small fortress from the octagonal turrets and narrow windows suitable for firing arrows at opponents. Besides the wonderful gatehouse and the ruins of the abbey beyond, there are an abundance of antique and specialty shops in the town.

### Battle Abbey
The gatehouse is considered one of the finest in the country and replaced an earlier gatehouse on the same site. It was built in 1338 by Abbott Retlynge and is complete with double archways, ribbed vaulting and portcullis through which the soldiers could defend their stronghold. The abbey fell during the Reformation under King Henry VIII, but part of it is now used as a school.

A tour of the Abbey ruins is assisted by an audiovisual account of the Battle of Hastings. The actual site of the battlefield between Harold and William the Conquerors' armies on Senlac Ridge is still clearly visible. The spot where King Harold died is indicated by a plaque stating, "...the victory of Duke William on 14 October 1066, the high altar was placed to mark the spot where King Harold died..."

There are many events held in and around the town of Battle. Call the Battle Tourist Information Center for more details.
Telephone: (0) 1424 773721. Address: High Street, Battle.

**1066 Country Walks**
The 1066 walk takes in the towns of Pevensey, Rye and Battle. There are links with other coastal villages and towns such as Bexhill-on-Sea and Hastings. The 1066 Country Walk is segmented into four parts allowing individuals to choose a walk as to their ability and interest. There are several brochures that can be obtained from the Battle Tourist Information of the walks, restaurants and even accommodation along the way.
Telephone: (0) 1424 773721. Address: High Street, Battle.

**Museum of Local History**
The museum is small but has some wonderful attractions. A copy of the Bayeux Tapestry, a battle scene of the fateful day on 1066, a copy of the Domesday Book as well as other interesting and unique items. There is also a history of the gunpowder industry that was so important to the livelihood of the town.
Telephone: (0) 1424 775955. Address: Memorial Hall, High Street, Battle.

## Food for thought:
### The Pilgrim's Rest Restaurant
The restaurant was built in the 14$^{th}$ century and was once an almshouse where the monks from the abbey distributed alms to the poor and gave spiritual guidance. It has changed hands and uses over the centuries but now provides wonderful meals to visitors. The specialties of the house are the savory pies, such as chicken and leek and steak and onion pies with a light and delicious crust. They are served with mountains of mashed potatoes and fresh vegetables. They also offer a splendid assortment of cakes, tarts and fruit pies that are homemade. The Pilgrim's Rest is located next to the gatehouse.
Telephone: 01424 772314. Address: 1, High Street, Battle.

## If you decide to stay:
### The George Hotel
The George is an elegant 19$^{th}$-century coaching hotel located in the center of the town and is ideally situated for sightseeing in Battle and the surrounding areas. The inn has an unusual oval, spiral staircase and 22 guest rooms, some with bathrooms en suite, a licensed bar and restaurant. Morning coffee and afternoon tea is also served.
Telephone: (0) 1424 774466. Address: 23 High Street, Battle.

## How to get there:
There is train service to Battle from London Bridge station.
**By car**: Take A21 south out of London to John's Cross, where you take the A2100 to Battle. Battle is approximately 62 miles away from central London

# Lewes

Anne of Cleves was sent from Germany to England to be the 4th wife of King Henry VIII. It was an arranged marriage designed to form a political alliance between the two countries and thus provide stability for England and mainland Europe. The king had never set eyes on his proposed bride but it was rumored that Anne's beauty rivaled the duchess of Milan whose loveliness was legendary. In spite of this, Henry had the painter Holbein provide a likeness of Anne so that he could see her beauty for himself. The painting seems to have satisfied the king's curiosity concerning her looks and the marriage was quickly arranged. When Henry saw Anne for the first time he was polite but bitterly upset. He later referred to her as the "Flanders Mare." The ceremony took place as planned because contracts had been carefully drafted but Anne knew she had made a terrible mistake. It was obvious to everyone that Henry was unhappy with the union since he had divorced his first wife, had his second beheaded and lost his third during childbirth. Anne feared for her life.

The arrangements for the wedding fell on Cromwell's shoulders, who arranged to have Hampton Court redecorated and ordered fine silks and cloth of gold for the courtiers who would attend the reception. Anne left her home in Düsseldorf and traveled overland to Calais where a ship took her across the English Channel to Dover. On her arrival in England, Anne was taken to Canterbury, where she was greeted by gentlewomen dressed in brightly-colored clothes of velvet and silk and bonnets trimmed with pearls. Anne must have felt embarrassed in her plain and unattractive clothes that were described behind her back as "ugly apparel."

The king had been staying at Greenwich reading letters from friends and officials telling him that his beautiful betrothed was most anxious to meet him. Anne was due to arrive at Rochester on New Year's Day to prepare for the wedding, but the king was impatient and decided he could wait no longer to see his bride. He planned on surprising her as he had done with Katherine of Aragon over 20 years earlier, by bursting into her chambers pretending to be a manservant of the king. Henry believed this prank would scare and then amuse Anne as it had done with Katherine and her ladies-in-waiting. After the initial shock, they would then fall about laughing and the king would shower her with gifts.

Henry arrived at Rochester Abbey about noon on New Year's Day. His plan to catch the bride unawares was a dismal failure when Anne realized that it was not the king's manservant but the king himself who had paid her a visit. As she stood to greet him her hair hung in an unruly fashion, her clothes were unkempt and her hands were rough. It was not only the absence of promised beauty that disappointed the king but Anne also lacked the social graces required by a Queen of England. Her English was very poor and made the initial meeting difficult but despite his displeasure, the king embraced his new bride and lightly kissed her before he left.

Once back at Greenwich, the king voiced his disapproval of Anne to Cromwell. It was Cromwell after all who had arranged the marriage and help draft the agreement. The king told him that had he known of Anne's countenance, he would never have agreed to the marriage. It was not just her bad looks but also her lack of culture that made the king seriously doubt if his new wife was suitable to be the Queen of England. Cromwell insisted that Anne was an intelligent woman and merely lacked the skills that could be taught by her English gentlewomen and, once dressed in a beautiful gown and cap, could easily pass as one of the ladies in the court.

As the wedding day approached the king became more apprehensive and told Cromwell, "...if it were not to satisfy the world and my realm, I would not do that I must do this date for none earthly thing." Even as Anne approached the king on her wedding day dressed in an exquisite gown decorated with pearls and jewels, the king found her unattractive and undesirable. The thought of the wedding night loomed in the back of his mind but not in the happy state of previous occasions when he took such delight in his new bride — one who might hopefully produce many sons. On this occasion, he was reluctant to take his bride to the bedchamber and when he did so he was sorely disappointed. He later described her body to his gentlemen friends as being unlike a maiden of 24 years and even questioned her virginity.

As the weeks turned into months the king became more despondent and searched for an end to the fruitless marriage. The marriage had never been consummated and therefore, in Henry's eyes, the marriage should be annulled.

Anne was fully aware of the danger she was in and searched desperately for a solution. If she returned to her homeland in disgrace, her brother would never forgive her and she would be considered a burden for the rest of her life. There would be no offers of marriage after the king's rejection and she would forever be the cause of many cruel jokes that would surely follow after such a public scandal. Anne considered her options and decided to appeal directly to the king and propose a solution to their difficult dilemma. She showed extraordinary skill and diplomacy in a letter she wrote to him on July 11, 1540, suggesting a possible remedy. It is said the king was most impressed with the letter which stated, "…that your highness will take me for your sister; for the which I most humbly thank you accordingly…"

The indebted king was eternally grateful for the diplomacy she used in the proceedings allowing him a quick divorce. As part of his gratitude, the king provided her a house in Lewes, two maidservants and a cook as well as many other benefits. Anne was pleased with the outcome and it is said she took a liking to English beer and became robust and contented throughout her life. She did indeed become a sister figure to the king and some would say a confidant and friend who encouraged him to see more of his children, for which he was most grateful.

During his marriage to Anne, Henry had become smitten with a young, flirtatious girl at court called Catherine Howard. Catherine was almost 30 years his junior but he was in love again and referred to her as "His rose without a thorn." The love match was the talk of the courtiers as they watched him behave foolishly, giving Catherine fine jewels and furs and trying to behave like a young man. Nobody guessed that he would take her as his 5th wife, but she would break his heart and then she would lose her head.

## **What to see and do today:**
Lewes is the county town of East Sussex and as such, is the administrative and social center of the county. The

narrow and twisting streets (or "twittens") still dominate the heart of the medieval town. After the Norman Conquest in 1066, Lewes was given to William De Warenne, who fought alongside William during the invasion. Warren had been one of a handful of Norman knights who believed William had the capability to bring together thousands of Norman knights, their horses and armor and cross the English Channel to invade England.

Lewes is an ancient town, rich with tile-hung medieval houses and interesting streets full of historic shops selling antiques, rare books and works of art. The river Ouse runs through the town and there are wonderful walks and peaceful gardens to explore such as the Grange and Southover. This walled garden has a variety of beautiful flowers, carefully tended and enhanced by the Winterbourne stream that runs through it.

The famous Glyndebourne Opera House, Anne of Cleves house, Southover gardens and Lewes Castle are all within easy reach from the town's center, as are the cellars of the Town Hall (originally The Star Inn) where 17 Protestant martyrs were kept until their death on June 22, 1557. They are remembered each year on November 5th with the infamous Guy Fawkes whose aborted effort to blow up the Houses of Parliament and bring down the Protestant king are celebrated with bonfires and fireworks. On the evening of November 5, members of the town climb the steps of the Town Hall with lighted torches held aloft and remember the men and women who are said to have climbed the steps to their death in a communal fire.

**Lewes Castle**
The castle is located at the north end of the town just off the High Street. William de Warren built the castle on instructions from the Duke of Normandy after he had con-

quered Britain. It was a strong fortress capable of withstanding the most severe of attacks but it also has a romantic feel with a bowling and jousting green. The Barbican (or reinforced gate house), which is at the entrance to the castle, is now a museum and houses many interesting artifacts excavated from the grounds and also the town itself. Many special events are held at the castle each year, and visitors should call for details.
Open: Monday through Saturday 10:00 a.m. until 5:00 p.m. Sunday 11:00 a.m. until 5:00 p.m.
Telephone: (0) 1273 486290. Address: 169 High Street, Lewes.

**Southover Grange and Gardens**
The Grange was built in the 16th century from stone taken from a nearby priory site and is nestled in the beautiful gardens at Southover. The public garden is surrounded by an ancient brick wall behind which is a peaceful and quiet sanctuary from the hustle and bustle of the town. There are carefully laid out flower beds, lawns and some unusual rose bushes and shrubs including a North American Tulip Tree. This garden is a perfect place to sit and have a picnic lunch under one of the archways, listening to the water from the Winterbourne stream as it passes through the middle of the park.

**Anne of Cleves House**
Henry VIII gave Anne the house on Southover Street as part of their divorce settlement. Although the house has been renovated over the last 400 centuries, it still retains the spectacular vaulted ceiling rafters of wood and the oak furnished main chamber. It is a beautiful house, full of character and charm, especially in the kitchen. The pretty and romantic garden has an abundance of roses and sweet aroma of herbs.

Telephone: (0) 1273 474610. January 2 through February 17, Tuesday, Thursday and Saturday 10:00 a.m. until 5:00 p.m. Sunday 12:00 noon until 5:00 p.m.
February 19 through November 4, Monday through Saturday 10:00 a.m. until 5:00 p.m.
Sunday 12:00 noon until 5:00 p.m.
November 6 through December 23, Tuesday through Saturday 10:00 a.m. until 5:00 p.m. Sunday 12:00 noon until 5:00 p.m.

**Bull House**
Tom Paine, an interesting and complex man, lived in Bull House in Lewes and earned his living as excise officer. After leaving Lewes, he moved to London and then on to Philadelphia where he became a journalist. He published an article on the abolition of slavery and, in 1776, he published the famous pamphlet entitled *Common Sense*, in which he criticized the British Parliament and argued for America's independence. Other famous people who lived at Bull House are Gideon Mantell, the 19th-century geologist, and John Harvard, who married a local girl and later founded Harvard University.

Bull House is now the home of the Sussex Archaeological Society and is not open to the public, however, it is an interesting house built in 1583 and the architecture is worth seeing if only from the exterior.

**The Star Inn (now the Town Hall)**
On the death of Henry VIII, his only son Edward VI (from Jane Seymour) became king at the age of 10 under the guidance of his uncle, the Duke of Somerset. He reigned for six years until he succumbed to tuberculosis in 1553. Since he was childless, Edward named Lady Jane Grey as his successor but she only managed to survive as queen for nine days. She was beheaded along with her husband.

During this time, Mary, Henry's first daughter by Catherine of Aragon, boldly marched on London to take the crown she believed was rightfully hers. She proved to be a tyrannical monarch intent on reviving Catholicism and reputedly was responsible for having more people burned at the stake than all her predecessor's put together, earning her the name "Bloody Mary." A total of 286 men and women were burned at the stake during her reign. In 1557 in Lewes alone she had 17 men and women burned because they would not renounce their Protestant beliefs. These 17 Protestant martyrs were kept in the cellars of the old Star Inn, now the Town Hall, and paraded through the town before climbing the steps of the Town Hall to their deaths. They are remembered each year on November 5th as part of the Guy Fawkes celebration.

## Food for thought:
### The Old Needlemakers Café
The café is located on West Street and Market Lane and provides anything from a morning cup of coffee to a delicious lunch or afternoon tea. There are many shops close by including an antiques center, candle and bookshops. There is a group called the Lewes Artisans whose works of art are sold in shops around the town.
Telephone: (0) 1273 486258/472322. Address: Market Lane, Lewes.

## If you decide to stay:
### The White Hart Hotel
The charming White Hart hotel is located in the center of Lewes. It was built in the 16th century as a coaching inn, but has been renovated over the centuries and is run by a local family. There are 52 guest rooms, an indoor swimming pool, sauna, steam room, gym and a spa bath. It is believed that Tom Paine and John Harvard used the inn

for their meetings before they left for America and began a new life.
Telephone: (0) 1273 476694. Address: High Street, Lewes.

**Berkeley House Hotel**
The hotel has been completely restored to its former beauty and elegance of a Georgian town house. It has five guest rooms available, singles and doubles and a wonderful terrace on the roof that provides an excellent view of the Downs. The hotel is in a great location for most of the sightseeing in town and the surrounding areas.
Telephone: (0) 1273 476057. Address: 2 Albion Street, Lewes.

## For more information:
Lewes Tourist Information Center.
Telephone: (0) 1273 483448. Address: 187 High Street, Lewes.

## How to get there:
There is direct train service from London Victoria to Lewes.
By car: Take A22 south out of London to Uckfield. About 2 miles south of Uckfield take the A26 directly to Lewes. Lewes is approximately 57 miles away from central London.

# Alfriston

The legend of St. Lewinna, a young Saxon virgin, began in the 7th century. She was just a girl bordering on womanhood when pagan Saxons took her body and life. Her broken body was taken to a nearby church where her remains were kept for centuries. It was rumored that those who made pilgrimage to the site of her remains were miraculously cured of their afflictions and had their prayers answered. Testimonials of the miracles performed adorned the walls of the little wooden church. A Flemish monk called Balgerus who visited the church by accident on Easter Monday stole the bones of St. Lewinna and took them back to Flanders because she appeared before him and said, "Rise, take me to yourself. Have me, I say, for the companion of your journey."

In 1058, a monk called Balgerus left his monastery in Dunkirk, France and traveled across the sea to England to help convert the pagans to Christianity. He arrived on the mainland at an unknown location on Easter Monday. Aware that he needed to observe the day with a special service, he traveled inland looking for a church. He came upon the small wooden church of St. Lewinna and spoke with the custodian, who gave a full account of the virgin Lewinna, the miracles and the answered prayers. The priest was intrigued by the stories of hundreds of pilgrims who traveled for days to obtain a cure. He was ashamed to admit that he secretly desired to possess them.

The custodian left the church briefly, believing he could safely leave the priest alone with the remains of St. Lewinna. Balgerus prayed for guidance; should he leave the relics that had remained in the church for over 400 years, or transport them to his home in Flanders? It was a difficult decision and the priest struggled with the sense of right and wrong but then, according to Balgerus, the saint appeared to him and suggested he take the bones to his town across the sea. He hurriedly collected the bones together in a sack but as he did so, the bones from St. Lewinna's fingers fell to the ground. Three times he tried to collect the bones together and each time he dropped them to the church floor. Taking this as an omen that the saint wanted some remains left at the church, he left the finger bones behind.

Balgerus clutched the bones of St. Lewinna to his chest and hurried back to his boat, afraid the villagers would discover the theft and pursue him. The captain and crew were waiting to depart but a storm had begun and the group was not anxious to take to sea. Once again it is said St. Lewinna appeared and indicated the journey would be safe and without incident, and the sailing party departed the shores of England. During the following weeks, Balgerus paraded the relics around the towns of Flanders holding them aloft for all to see. It is believed that pilgrimages began immediately, and those who traveled to visit the remains had the same miraculous cures bestowed upon them as those in the little town in England.

Some evidence shows the legend may be true because in the 11th century, the relics of St. Lewinna turned up in Bergues in Flanders. During the 16th century, the town was ransacked and burned, allegedly destroying the remains. However, a small sliver of bone, believed to be from one of St. Lewinna's ribs, is still kept in a silver vault.

During the Middle Ages and through medieval times, there were many instances of relics having been collected from holy origins. Bones, teeth, stones and blood-soaked pieces of wood supposedly from important people and events have been housed in churches or cathedrals for centuries, bringing pilgrims who prayed for a miracle cure. However, it has been proven that some of the relics were in fact faked, because on examination they were found to be the blood and bones of animals.

Other legends and tales from the area are of smugglers along and around the coast of East Sussex. The Alfriston Gang with its notorious leader, Stanton Collins, caused havoc for years until he and his gang were eventually captured and sent to the colonies or executed.

Another name for smugglers was "owlers," and some believe Collins was the leader of the "owling fraternity." The owlers, fearful the Customs' men would turn the smugglers against each other, began the fraternity where each man swore an allegiance to the group. Penalty for divulging members' names or locations of booty to the authorities was a slow and painful death administered by group members. The lucrative wool market brought the inevitable taxes and duties, which in turn encouraged groups of smugglers to spring up all over the country, particularly on the coastline of East Sussex. The Crown believed the wool trade to be so important to the livelihood of the country that they placed a penalty of death on any smuggler found guilty of outward smuggling. As a reminder of the importance of the wool trade and the prosperity it brought to the country, the Chancellor in the House of Lords still sits on a large "wool sack" to this day.

Records show that James Collins, a butcher, purchased the Market Cross House in Alfriston in 1815. When James died in 1823, he left his home and business to his son Stanton whom he had trained as a butcher with the intent that he would continue the family trade. Unfortunately, the smuggling of wool proved a more lucrative market for Stanton and he was soon involved with a group of unsavory individuals who not only smuggled but also poached. Many men in the area felt the act of poaching a privilege, not a crime that was punishable by a 7-year term in the Colonies. There is some evidence to suggest that Stanton conspired with others who stole sheep and poached game by using his skill as a butcher to turn carcasses into neat bundles of meat that were difficult for the authorities to determine their origin.

It was not only the smuggling but also the contraband from shipwrecks that caused the Customs' men to seek out the local owlers. The owlers would watch for a shipwreck and then take a small boat or wade out to collect the barrels of rum and boxes of personal effects. They were tough, strong men capable of defending themselves against attack by the coast guards in their fast sailing cutters. Sometimes the smugglers had to travel several miles inland to store their plunder in barns and inns around the countryside. Even though the lights from their torches made a beacon for the customs men to follow, they did not always do so, having been bribed with a barrel or two of rum.

Collins was eventually convicted of stealing grain and barley and was transported to the Colonies in 1831. Possibly this was the only offense that could be proven against him by the courts, for although he did mix with a corrupt group of men, his supposed smuggling activities could not be proven. Other gang members were not so lucky. The Huggett brothers were transported in 1836, accused of highway robbery and sentenced to 7 years' hard labor, and another member, Thorncraft, was hanged because of his complicity in an act of arson.

Market Cross House (now the Smuggler's Inn) once had 6 staircases, 48 doors and 21 rooms, many with concealed doorways, secret passages and tunnels. Most of the doors held heavy bolts and latches, possibly to stop unwelcome visitors. It is believed there is a secret tunnel from the Smugglers Inn to a distant location although no evidence has been found to substantiate this claim.

## What to see and do today:

The town of Alfriston is nestled in the South Downs and around the Cuckmere River. It is a delightful place full of interesting homes, historical buildings and little shops full of wonderful souvenirs and keepsakes. In 1405, Henry IV granted a charter for the town to hold a weekly market and two annual fairs. A charter was a valuable means of commerce because nearby villagers would come to sell their farm produce and ply their trades, therefore bringing prosperity to the town. There used to be a tannery making gloves, a chandler and a rope maker in the village. The importance of these trades and the prosperity they brought to the town is depicted on the village sign on the green known locally as the Tye.

### St. Andrew's Church

The original site of St. Andrews was close to Weavers Lane and King's Ride. It was believed to be the place where St. Lewinna's church had stood centuries ago. While building the new church, a strange event took place. As the workmen returned to work each morning, they noticed the foundation stones had been disturbed overnight and flung about the green. On another occasion, four oxen were found rump-to-rump, forming a cross on the Tye. Believing this to be a good omen, the workmen began new foundations for St. Andrew's church on this very spot. The work began in 1360, and was built all at one time rather than added to over centuries as with many other churches. It is a large and beautiful church and is known as the "Cathedral of the Downs."

**The Clergy House**
The Clergy House is a 14th-century timber-framed house close to the church. During the 15th century the Michelham Priory purchased the home and owned it for the next 500 years. Eventually the home fell into disrepair and was purchased in 1896 by a new organization called The National Trust, and was completely refurbished it to its present state. The Clergy House was the first building to be purchased by the National Trust.
Open: Daily 10:00 a.m. until 5:00 p.m. (except Tuesday and Friday) from April through October.
Telephone: (0) 1323 870001. Address: High Street, Alfriston.

**Recommended Walks**
There are several walks from the town to the surrounding countryside. The most adventurous is a three-mile walk on the west bank of the Cuckmere, south to Cuckmere Haven and the Seven Sisters Country Park. Depending on your ability to hike, the journey will take about 1½ to 2 hours.

Another and less strenuous walk would be to the hamlet of Lullington. This journey takes about 30 to 45 minutes and is approximately 1 mile from Alfriston.

# Food for thought:
## The Smugglers Inn
The Smugglers Inn is a delightful place to visit and eat. There are many exposed wooden beams throughout, with low ceilings and nooks. The fireplace is huge, with insets for people to sit (or hide). The owners speculate there is a hidden doorway in the chimney to a staircase leading to the rooms above. There is a poster on the wall giving the Rules of the House from 1734: "Hand in your pistols, cudgels and knives. There will be no swearing; no touching of the wenches; no banging of the tankards on the tables. To stay overnight will cost a shilling; your horse will cost 4 pennies."

The food at the Smugglers Inn is traditional with a great Ploughman's lunch consisting of several different types of cheese, pickles, tomatoes and crusty bread.
Telephone: (0) 1323 870241. Address: High Street, Alfriston.

# If you decide to stay:
## Dean's Place Hotel
Dean's Place Hotel was built in the 14th century and has been renovated over the centuries. It is located on 5 acres of beautifully landscaped gardens surrounded by the rolling countryside of Sussex. The hotel has a croquet lawn, heated outdoor swimming pool and a mini putting green. The South Downs Way, a popular hiking trail is within 100 yards of the hotel and links up with other rambler trails around the surrounding areas. The hotel is part of The Best Western hotel group and offers 36 guest rooms.
Telephone: (0) 1323 870248. Address: Seaford Road, Alfriston.

**The Star Inn**
The Star Inn was one of four inns in Alfriston and is thought to have been built in the 14th century. A large Dutch wooden figurehead sits on the outside of the inn and is reputedly from a shipwreck in the Cuckmere Haven. Stanton Collins, who most likely plundered the contents of the ship and took the figurehead as a trophy, brought it to the town where it has remained. Also on the outside of The Star are several carvings on the wood. Saint Michael is seen fighting a dragon that has an eye in its tail, a bishop with an animal at his feet and Saint Julian, a patron saint of travelers.

The Star Inn has been renovated over the past few years but has retained its charming character and is considered one of the oldest hostelries in the country. The inn is half-timbered with an overhanging upper level and tiny lead windows. The landlord boasts of providing the finest ales and beers, great pub food as well as traditional English meals. The guest rooms are said to be comfortably furnished, in keeping with the character of the inn. Telephone: (0) 8704 0088102. Address: High Street, Alfriston.

## Neighboring places of interest:
### Lullington
The little church of Lullington can be seen nestled in the Downs surrounded by trees in the Cuckmere Valley. It is a tiny church measuring 16 feet square and can only support a congregation of approximately 20 people. However, during the Harvest Festival, it has held more than 40 parishioners. The church was built in the 13th century and belonged to Battle Abbey for some time. It has changed hands often over the centuries and has been referred to many times. In 1521, an individual called Jegelian Hunt bequeaths items to the church "...I will a taper sett before

Saint Sithe in the same church." It is not known whom Saint Sithe was but could have been Saint Sitha, Saint Citha or Saint Zita, patron saint of housemaids, homemakers and people ridiculed for their piety. Saint Zita had been a domestic servant for a family in Lucca, Italy and had been in service since she was a child of 12 years. She was a generous and loving person who often gave her own food and sometimes that of the household to the poor and needy in the town. Her master often reprimanded Zita, but the people of the town loved her and eventually she was given sainthood for her kindly deeds.

It is believed that a replica of Lullington Church was built in the United States as a war memorial but the actual location is unknown since the architect agreed not to disclose its whereabouts.

## How to get there:
There is no direct train service to Alfriston; however, it is possible to travel from London Victoria to Lewes, from where Alfriston can be reached by taxi.

**By car**: Take A22 south out of London to Uckfield and then on to Polegate. Take A27 west and look for signs on your left to Alfriston. Alfriston is approximately 58 miles away from central London.

# Wilmington

It is believed that it was the Celts, the ancient Britons, who first began creating the figures we see carved on the hillsides of England. The mysterious Long Man of Wilmington, carved into a nearby hillside, probably dates back to those times. Viewed from the air, he is seen elongated with a staff in each hand, but from the ground, he appears to be in perfect proportion. He is one of the largest human images in the world, measuring 226 feet tall, and is second only to a giant in Chile who measures 393 feet. Some believe the Long Man was originally cut in the chalk hillside as an emblem of cult worship, or possibly a fertility figure or an early surveyor. Others believe he was merely used as a landmark to guide travelers towards Wilmington.

In 1710, a drawing of the Long Man depicts him holding staves in both hands, as he is seen today, but both feet are pointing outward and he has facial features. It is believed that his feet once pointed downward and that he wore a headdress in the form of some kind of plume. There are many theories about his origin, especially as he sits on a ley line and is the third of five important sites located on this particular ley that runs SSW-NNE for approximately two miles.

Leys are believed to be ancient paths across the country linking one significant site to another. They are often more discernible from the air than the ground, and pilots sometimes use them for orientation purposes guiding them towards their destination. In ancient times, travelers depended upon sight and communication to locate a particular village or church. Therefore, a physical marker was necessary to guide them. This could be in the form of a large stone (landmark), piles of stones (cairn), or a group of trees. The long life of the yew tree made it a favorite landmark by the ancient Britons who felt these trees also had spiritual connotations.

There are five sites of interest on the ley that begins in Friston Forest. The first site is at the south end. It is a tumulus that is difficult to find because of the dense overgrowth. The second site is a round barrow measuring approximately 135 feet in diameter, which is believed to have contained an urn that was placed on a pile of flints. The third marker on the ley is the Long Man. The fourth point of interest is the priory at Wilmington. Norman Benedictine monks built it in the early 12th century, although it is thought there was a previous pagan church on the site because a stone head was found in the loose masonry and is believed to be of Celtic origin. The fifth and last site on the ley is the church of St. Mary and St. Peter, also built in the 12th century.

There are many theories and speculations regarding the origin of leys since they run in straight lines and will often take a traveler over a hill rather than perhaps an easier route around it. Some people believe that UFOs have traveled along ley lines, following some kind of magnetic earth force or energy that emits from them. It is also thought that animals can "feel" the energy or earth force, which encourages them to congregate in certain spots in a field or meadow.

Leys often run through a burial site such as a barrow or burial mound. Mysterious stone circles or megaliths often marked a particular route or pathway. Many of these circles tend to be on high, remote areas in the countryside and appear to display a surprisingly good knowledge of astronomy, particularly concerning the movements of the moon and sun. The mysteries of ley lines are not confined just to the English countryside; they can be found in many other parts of the world. As in England, they appear to be better seen from the air, leading to speculations about the origin. In Peru, there are many shrines located along straight tracks that radiate from the Temple of the Sun in Cuzco.

The Long Man is host to several groups of people who visit him regularly. The Morris Men perform their dances at the site, while the White Witches of East Sussex meet every few months to perform their rituals, especially during harvest and other specific holidays. They are a large group whose main interest is the land and Mother Nature's influence on the seasons.

There is another chalk figure called the White Horse that is cut into a hill in Litlington, East Sussex. Once again, the figure is cut into the hillside exposing the chalk and depicts a huge prancing horse. The Sussex Archaeological Society maintains the site.

## What to see and do today:
### The Village
The name of Wilmington is believed to have originated from the Saxon word Wilma-ing-ton, homestead of Wilma. It is a small village, really no more than a hamlet, with an ancient history. There are many old buildings in the village called the Chantry, Sanctuary and Fairleigh but the oldest house is probably Hunters Dene, that was most likely built in 1450.

Three stone heads have been found in Wilmington. They appear to be Celtic, and two of them were found in the ancient church and priory. The third head is located at the Chantry in the village. It is unusual to find several stone heads such as these, and this has led to many unanswered questions concerning their origin.

**The Long Man**
The Long Man has puzzled scholars for centuries with speculations that he was perhaps of Roman origin. He is carved on the north face of Windover Hill in a beautiful combe, a hollow in a hillside, with his arms outstretched in a non-aggressive poise. During excavations, some pieces of Roman tile were found in the trenches around the giant. It was this find that led to the speculation that perhaps it was the Romans who first cut the figure in the likeness of a standard bearer. A similar image can be seen on the reverse side of 4$^{th}$-century Roman coins found in Britain and also on a 7$^{th}$-century Saxon brooch.

One of the most popular theories is that the giant was a fertility figure whose personal features were removed during the Puritan era. His shape has certainly changed over the centuries for one reason or another, but many couples still visit the giant in the hopes that, by some strange coincidence, he could help them conceive.

During World War II, it was feared that the giant would be a target for the German Luftwaffe or at the least give them a point of reference. At this time, he was painted with green paint so was known as the Green Man for many years.

The maintenance of the Long Man was once the duty of the local Boy Scout troop, but this was considered an unsuitable activity for the boys. The responsibility of maintaining the figure went to the South Downs Conservation Board and the Morris Dancers.

The Long Man Morris Men perform many traditional dances from around the area, but they have written and designed a special dance for the Long Man. They perform this dance on May Day at dawn, dressed in their traditional garb. The dances are for groups of six to eight men who use sticks or handkerchiefs and music from the melodeon or pipe and tabor. They wear black top hats, white shirts with a collar, black waistcoats and breeches, white socks and black shoes. They also wear baldricks, which are crossed bands over their chests with bells above their elbows and below their knees.
Telephone: (0) 1273 588193. The Squire, Long Man Morris Men.

**St. Mary and St. Peter's Church**
Construction of the church of St. Mary and St. Peter began in the 12th century on what is believed to have been a previous pagan site. Some renovations have been made over the centuries but the church still retains its original character and charm. Access to the church is through the 14th-century porch, and the 13th-century north chapel, which is now a vestry and houses a spectacular stained-glass window called the "Bee and Butterfly Window." The window is quite beautiful and portrays St. Peter encircled with various butterflies and other insects.

A wonderful, old yew tree stands in the grounds of the churchyard, and is believed to be almost 2,000 years old. It measures approximately 23 feet in circumference and is braced by props and chains to keep it alive. Yew trees were often planted over a natural spring and were used during pagan rituals and cult worship.

**Wilmington Priory**

The Wilmington Priory was originally an outpost of the Benedictine Abbey of Nortre-Dame and was built in the 12th century. It was not built in the traditional style of a Benedictine abbey, as there were no cloisters or chapter houses, and was relatively small in comparison to other abbeys. The main purpose was to provide living accommodations to the prior and his monks who were custodians of the priory and surrounding land. As land agents, they would have kept a detailed account of any transactions that would have been sent to the parent house in Normandy.

The priory has undergone many renovations over the centuries but much of the original characteristics remain. The early 13th-century hall entrance still survives and the steps enter the additional wing that was built around the 14th century from the garden.

The ownership of the priory is now in the hands of the Landmark Trust, who rescue historic homes and buildings, restoring them to their former beauty. The buildings are then offered to the public for unique vacation accommodations.

## Food for thought:
### The Giant's Rest

The Giant's Rest is a family-owned business that prides itself on homemade meals. The owners are part of an organization called the Campaign for Real Food, who pride themselves on producing only food that is homemade and never purchase pre-packed foods. They have a great selection of meals from savory and fruit pies to pasta. They also offer a fine selection of wines from around the world and also local ales. The décor is best described as "Bistro" type, with church pews as seats and old rustic tables that

have antique bar games or wooden puzzles to amuse visitors.
Telephone: (0) 1323 870207. Address: The Street, Wilmington.

## If you decide to stay:
### Wilmington Priory
The Landmark Trust undertook the repairs and duty to restore the priory to its former beauty in 1999. They consulted an architectural firm who carefully created the custodian's quarters and six guest bedrooms that are available to the general public for accommodation. The interior design ranges from medieval to Victorian times, providing an interesting and historic journey through the life of the priory.
Telephone: (0) 1628 825925. Address: Wilmington Priory, Wilmington.

### Crossways Hotel
The Crossways hotel is ideally situated and only half a mile from the Southdowns and Weald Way. These are excellent hiking/walking trails and provide a wonderful opportunity to see the countryside on foot and enjoy the natural beauty. The hotel is nestled on two acres with mature trees, attractive gardens and a pond with resident ducks. It has seven guest bedrooms all with bathroom en suite, televisions, direct dial telephones as well as tea and coffee facilities. The owners strive to make a comfortable and enjoyable holiday for their visitors.
Telephone: (0) 1323 482455. Address: Wilmington, near Polegate.

## How to get there:
There is direct train service from London Victoria to Polegate, from which Wilmington may be reached by a short

taxi ride. Travel time is approximately 1 hour and 20 minutes.

**By car**: Take A21 south out of London to Uckfield. Just south of Uckfield take A22 to Polegate. In Polegate take A27 west to Wilmington. Wilmington is approximately 58 miles away from central London.

## Neighboring places of interest:
### Michelham Priory
Gilbert De l'Aigle founded the Michelham Priory in 1229 as part of the Augustinian Priory of the Holy Trinity. The Augustinian canons were ordained priests, not monks, and lived their lives in prayer and instruction of younger priests. They provided hospitality to travelers regardless of status, and hosted the Archbishop of Canterbury in 1283 and King Edward in 1302.

The canons of Michelham wore black habits and because of this were known as "black canons." Several members of the village, including a collector of rent, bakers, carters and cheese makers, assisted the canons. During the dissolution of the monasteries by Henry VIII, the canons were paid through March 25, 1537, and were allowed to take only their beds on their departure. The jewels and precious silver vessels were taken and sold, and the bells were sold to a brazier. Thomas Cromwell was given the priory estates to lease for a small sum of money but after he fell out of favor with the king and was beheaded, the priory and surrounding land was returned to the Crown.

The priory moat is one of the longest medieval water-filled moats in the country. It is over one mile in length and encircles almost seven acres of beautiful grounds. The gatehouse stands over 60 feet high with a small turret on the southeast corner. The turret holds the original spiral staircase leading to the upper levels and the roof. On each level, there is a latrine that overhangs the moat. The cloisters have a wonderful yew hedge on the north and east boundaries.

Herbert Pelham built the Tudor wing after he purchased the priory in 1587. The Child family purchased the property in 1791 and records show they had a thriving business of breeding cattle, brewing beer and making cider. The Child family were responsible for cross breeding and producing a specific breed of cattle called the "Sussex Reds," which took many prestigious 1st and 2nd places in stock shows.

The priory offers a glimpse into 800 years of history with a working watermill, a splendid Tudor mansion that is said to be haunted and a magnificent garden planted with an excellent herbaceous border. A Physic Garden shows the plants that were grown in order for the priests to administer to the sick as well as provide a practical use for the kitchen.
Open: 10:30 a.m. until 4:00 p.m. Closed on Mondays and Tuesdays. Wednesday through Sunday from middle of March until the end of October. Special Bank holiday events throughout the year. Call for specific opening details and information on the water mill and Great Barn. Telephone: (0) 1323 844224. Address: Michelham Priory, Upper Dicker, Hailsham.

# Pevensey

The comet streaked through the sky on April 24, 1066, and stayed in the night sky for 7 days. The monks called it cometa, the hairy star, but King Harold and the Witan believed it was a bad omen and that they were doomed. The Anglo-Saxon Chronicles mentions this event as William the Conqueror, otherwise known as the Duke of Normandy, amassed an army to invade England and take the crown he believed had been unjustly refused him. It would be the last time England was invaded and conquered, and it changed the lives of every Briton.

The key events that led to the invasion of England during the year of 1066 varies from Anglo-Saxon and Norman accounts but one thing is clear: William believed the crown of England was his and his alone. There is some evidence to suggest that Harold had met with William years earlier and implied that William's claim was appropriate since he was a distant cousin of King Edward the Confessor, whose marriage to Edith was childless. In any event, it had been clearly understood by William that he would inherit the crown when Edward died.

As King Edward lay dying on January 4, 1066, passing in and out of delirium, the Witan, a group of wise men that advised the king, pondered an heir. They believed their prayers had been answered when the king took Harold Godwin's hand and proclaimed, "...I also commend to you those men who have left their lands for love of me..." he then gave instructions for his burial. The comment could have meant he intended Harold to continue his lifelong devotion to the crown but the Witan seized the opportunity to place an Englishman on the throne. They prepared for the coronation the following day. It was be a short and turbulent reign that ended on the battlefield ten months later.

The news of Edward the Confessor's death and the hasty coronation of King Harold spread quickly across the channel. It is said that William was infuriated as he received the news and shut himself away for days as he pondered what should be done. He had made it known throughout Normandy that he would be crowned King of England and now that the crown had been refused him, he would be seen as a weak and ineffective leader.

During the next few weeks, envoys were dispatched back and forth across the channel suggesting the coronation had been a terrible mistake and that he, William, was ready to assume the responsibility of the monarchy. He reminded Harold that he had sworn on holy relics of his intention of placing William on the throne of England, but these pleas went unanswered.

The Normans were a particularly fierce and combative people. William's father, Robert I, Duke of Normandy, saw to it that his illegitimate young son, born as the result of his relationship with Arletta, the daughter of a tanner, would be trained as a skilled knight.

William was born in either 1027 or 1028. It is said that he was a difficult young man who often challenged authoritative figures. When he was very young, his father left Normandy to fight in the Holy Land. Before he departed, he spoke to his council and advised them that his son William was the rightful heir to the title of Duke of Normandy and although he was small, he would grow into a fine and worthy leader. He must have seen his own fate because he died on route to the Holy Land and young William inherited the title of Duke of Normandy.

The following years in Normandy were turbulent times and, with no strong leader to guide them, the barons took full advantage of the chaos. They began building personal armies to protect themselves and their assets. Influential families sent their sons off early in their lives to be trained as hardened knights, but most of them had no formal education and were illiterate. William's family protected him by placing him with various family members at secret locations. He bloomed early and showed an interest in politics and military affairs, taking the Truce of God when he was 14 years old. The Truce of God was a prelude to knighthood where specific guidelines of chivalry and honor were learned and sworn to uphold. He was knighted when he was only 16 years of age.

William distinguished himself as he fought for the King of France as his vassal. He showed that he was a ruthless and cruel man capable of inflicting terrible punishment on those who opposed him. Although illiterate, he was an extraordinary military tactician, which was not lost on the king. Over the following decades William became a strong leader and was well regarded by the knights of Normandy.

During this relatively harsh and combative time in Normandy, the English people had led a contented life under the reign of Edward the Confessor, who was not a strong monarch and left the guidance of the country in Harold's care. The people were reluctant to fight even if the king demanded it, as they had grown accustomed to living in harmony with their neighbors.

The Anglo-Saxons had laws that they firmly believed no man was above, even the king himself. There were also severe laws regarding weaponry such as the use of the bow and arrow. It was seen as a gentleman's sport and, therefore, not suitable for the regular soldier. The English soldiers fought hand-to-hand combat with swords and axes; even their horses were no more than shaggy ponies, normally used to carrying loads.

The Anglo-Saxon Chronicles and the Bayeux Tapestry describe the weeks following Harold's coronation. It is said that William sulked for some time and then decided he would attack England and seize the crown for himself. The chronicles describe how he courted the sympathetic barons of Normandy with promises of untold wealth if they joined him with their armies. Many agreed to accompany him, and he began to build an armada of considerable size, but some were skeptical since an endeavor of this magnitude had never been attempted. Crossing the channel was difficult under the best weather conditions, but to cross with thousands of men, their specially bred stallions, armory, food and water seemed ridiculous to contemplate.

It is not known whether William was aware that the Viking King of Norway, Harald Hardrada, also intended to invade Britain before the winter. It was September 25 and both invading armies were restless and eager for battle. Winter was looming and unless the weather turned in their favor soon, they would have to retreat and wait until the spring.

Harold heard that the Vikings had landed on the East Coast of England while he was in London and so set off at once, marching 195 miles north to Stamford Bridge. Harold and his men were victorious but they had little time to celebrate, as news came that William had landed at Pevensey. Harold immediately turned his army around and fast-marched them southward for a distance of 250 miles. The trek was accomplished in 13 days, an unbelievable military maneuver. During this time it was learned that William had the blessing of the church, and that the pope had excommunicated Harold. This lay heavily on Harold's shoulders, and it is believed that a change came over him as he traveled to Pevensey.

After landing at Pevensey, William marched his men six miles inland and camped for the night. It is said that William's army spent the evening in prayer while Harold's men drank beer, told stories and sang songs. At dawn the following morning on October 14, 1066, the two armies faced each other. Harold had the logistical advantage atop the Senlac ridge and had a larger army. The Norman soldiers fought as they had in Normandy; their expert archers filled the skies with waves of arrows that pierced the English troops' armor and they dropped by the hundreds. Still, the English army would not be deterred and they continued to move forward mounting a counterattack. Several Norman knights on horseback turned as if in retreat and some of Harold's men foolishly pursued them, leaving their posts unguarded. William immediately saw the tactical advantage and instructed others to do likewise causing more disruption to the English troops as they left their flanks unguarded.

The battle continued for the whole day and it is said the English were brave and met their death honorably. In a recent article in the Daily Mail, William was quoted as saying, "They stood firmly, as if fixed to the ground, the dead by falling, seemed to move more than the living." King Harold died alongside his men from an arrow in the eye and was then cut to ribbons by Norman knights because he was unable to defend himself.

William was crowned King of England on Christmas Day 1066, and he swore, as part of the coronation oath, to preserve the "good and ancient laws" of the Anglo-Saxon kings. Part of those laws was the tradition of calling several men to swear an oath endorsing a litigant's claim. This, in turn, developed into the jury system we see today.

William had promised himself that if he defeated Harold, he would build an abbey in his opponent's honor. After the triumphant battle, he kept his promise and built an abbey at Battle on the site where Harold lost his life. The two men were of similar age and it is believed they liked and respected each other. However, records tell us that William did not like the English people or the countryside and never tried to learn their language. He honored his commitment to the knights of Normandy who followed him into battle by awarding them various parts of England. They became the new gentry, married Anglo-Saxon women and settled down to a less combative life.

The Domesday Book (compilation of which began in 1086) documented every village, inhabitant, cattle and building upon which a tax could be levied. The sheriff collected the taxes that were presented to the Treasurer on a table covered with a checkered cloth, eventually leading to the title of Chancellor of the Exchequer used today. The people of England were so afraid of the information collected in the book that they called it The Domesday Book after God's final day of judgment.

William spent very little time in the country after the invasion, preferring to leave the administration to his half brother, Bishop Odo. He returned to Normandy and fought with the king whom he had served as a vassal.

It is suggested by chronicles of the day that William was unhappy at the outcome of the battle with Harold, and that he was impressed with the loyalty and dedication of the English men to their king. William had conquered Britain but not the people who remained defiant and stubborn. On his deathbed, he repented his treatment of the English people but they never forgave him for the cruel punishment he inflicted. They also refused to learn the French language and assimilate Norman customs. They were defiant in every way but one thing was sure, life in England changed forever.

## What to see and do today:
### Pevensey Castle

The strategic location of Pevensey was not lost on William the Conqueror or the Romans before him. The castle was one of many Shore Forts that were built by the Romans throughout England, and William simply used what was left of the castle for his own purposes. He gave the stronghold to Bishop Odo, who built a castle of his own within the walls of the Roman structure.

The castle walls are more than 12 feet thick in places and there are still walls over 20 feet high today, giving an excellent idea of what the castle would have looked like a 1,000 years ago. Pevensey castle has a moat that made a frontal attack and underground assault almost impossible. The most common way to attack an apparently impregnable castle was be to mine underground. The men were called sappers or miners who tunneled towards the castle wall or tower, shoring the tunnel as they went with posts impregnated with hog grease. Once the tunnel was completed, the posts and other combustible materials were set alight; causing an inferno that would collapse the wall or tower and provide access to the castle.

The village of Pevensey is small, with several half-timbered and flint houses. In addition to being an ancient town mentioned in the Domesday Book, the Romans inhabited the town between A.D. 250 and 300. When the Romans abandoned the village around A.D. 408, the Anglo-Saxons seized the castle.
Open: Daily 10:00 a.m. until 5:00 p.m. from March to October and from October to March from Wednesday until Sunday 10:00 a.m. until 5:00 p.m.

**The Tudor Mint House (Antique Shop)**
The mint stands close to the walls of the castle and is believed to be where the first coins were struck during William's reign. It is also mentioned in the Domesday Book. The original building is rumored to have had a secret passage that led from the castle to the mint as men carried the products back and forth. Coins were struck at this site through the reigns of William the Conqueror, William Rufus, Henry I and King Stephen from 1076 until 1154. Several of the coins minted at this location are exhibited at the British Museum and other museums around the country.

The present building was built in 1342 and is a splendid half-timbered house with dark red tiles and overhanging eaves. It is rumored to be haunted by a young woman who was the mistress of Thomas Dight, who rented the house. Dight returned home unexpectedly one evening to find his lady in the arms of another man. Retribution was swift and the poor girl died slowly and painfully; it is her ghost that appears dressed in a close-fitted dress and a ruffle around her neck.

The Old Mint Antique Shop is one of the largest wholesale antique distributors in the country, and they ship worldwide. They have approximately 10,000 items in the shop

and warehouse behind the property. The merchandise changes frequently and offers a wide display of antiques of every kind.
Telephone: (0) 762337. Address: High Street, Pevensey.

### Court House and Gaol
It is said to be the smallest town hall in England, with the gaol on the ground floor and the courtroom above. The courthouse is now a museum and is only open at special times for viewing. Call for details.
Telephone: (0) 1323 411400. Eastbourne Tourist Information Center.

### 1066 Walks
The 1066 walk from Pevensey Castle via Battle and on to Rye is a 31-mile hike through the countryside that William himself walked after he landed at Pevensey. The walk can be broken into smaller segments with refreshments or even accommodations en route. There are several brochures available from the tourism office that advises walkers of the points of historic interest, flora and wildlife.
Telephone: (0) 1424 781111. Hastings Tourist Information Center.

## Food for thought:
### The Smugglers Inn
The Smugglers Inn was built in 1541 on the main road in Pevensey. It is listed on the official ghost tour of Pevensey but the landlord has never seen a ghost. The inn has retained the character and charm of centuries passed with low ceilings, heavily wooden beams and two fireplaces. It is decorated with traditional horse brasses, unusual china plates and accessories. The inn serves a wonderful roast dinner on Sundays as well as a varied menu throughout the week. It is a favorite for the local people in winter, with

a roaring fireplace, and in summer when the beer garden is used.
Telephone: (0) 1323 762112. Address: High Street, Pevensey.

## If you decide to stay:
### The Smugglers Inn
The Smugglers Inn has three guest bedrooms, all with bathrooms en suite, tea or coffee facilities and televisions in each room. The rooms are decorated in a soft, comfortable style and kept in character with the low ceilings, small windows and wood-beamed ceilings and walls. A traditional English breakfast is served each morning and an evening meal can be arranged on request.
Telephone: (0) 1323 762112. Address: High Street, Pevensey.

## How to get there:
There is direct train service from London Victoria to Pevensey. Travel time is approximately 1 hour and 45 minutes.
**By car**: Take A21 south out of London to Hastings. In Hastings take A259 west directly to Pevensey. Pevensey is approximately 63 miles away from central London.

# Ringmer

The Peasants' Revolt of 1381 started in Brentwood, Essex and quickly spread to Kent and East Sussex. The men of Ringmer played an important part in this rebellion, as they would again later during the Civil War and the Captain Swing riots in the 19th century. Certain women of Ringmer also shared this spirited nature. Ann Sadler married John Harvard in 1636 and Gulielma Springett married William Penn in 1672. The two couples left England in search of adventure and a life free from religious persecution in the New World.

The Hundred Years War (1337–1453) between England and France had greatly diminished the British coffers and a new tax, the third in four years, known as the Poll Tax, came into effect. The burden fell directly on the poor, who could least afford an increase, but also on the landowners and gentry. A particularly bad episode of the Black Death had killed between one-third and one-half of the population, and those able-bodied men who survived felt empowered for the first time in their lives. They believed the severe labor shortage gave them the opportunity to demand higher wages and possibly abolish serfdom altogether.

The unrest of the villagers continued to escalate and in 1381, the peasants were joined by wealthy landowners and outspoken ministers like John Ball and Jack Straw. The clergymen sided with the rebels in their demand for lower taxes and better living conditions. But it was another man, Wat Tyler who emerged as the natural leader and spokesman for the peasants. He was a blacksmith by trade and fully understood the needs of the people he represented. Wat Tyler and a group of peasants marched on London with a petition they intended to submit to the king if he would grant them an audience.

Richard II had been crowned king in 1377 at the tender age of 10 years and had ruled the country under the guidance of his uncle, John of Gaunt. Now at 14 years of age, he was ready to assume the responsibilities of the crown and prove to his people that he was a fair and just monarch. The meeting with Tyler would be a challenge to his authority and power, but he relished the opportunity. Soon word came that the rebels had descended on the City of London and burned the Savoy Palace, home of John of Gaunt. They then set fire to the Treasurer's manor and burned any legal documents they could find. They stormed the jails and released the prisoners regardless of their crimes, and these men also joined the riot. Despite these actions, the young king still agreed to meet with Tyler.

On June 14, 1381, King Richard and a small group of his lords met Tyler at Mile End, London, and listened to the petition of the peasants. They pledged their allegiance to the king if he would agree to their demands for the abolition of villeinage and the right to rent land at four pence an acre. At first the king agreed to their demands but then Tyler became obnoxious and insulted the king. This infuriated the Mayor of London who drew his sword and struck the militant Tyler. He staggered a few feet and collapsed but rose again and was then attacked and killed by the king's men. Then it is said the young monarch stood and addressed the assembly telling them to go home peacefully saying, "Your leader is dead. Follow me; I am your leader."

Instead of leaving London, some of the rebels continued the riot by storming the Tower of London and taking the Archbishop of Canterbury, the Chancellor, and John of Gaunt's physician as prisoners. They considered these men the principals in their continued suppression and so took them to the green at the Tower and murdered them. As a result of this action, the king renounced his pledge to honor the peasants' petition. John Ball was hanged during the summer of 1381. Many men who participated in the riot were hunted down and executed, but others went quietly home and resumed their everyday lives.

The rioting continued in many towns around the country where villagers burned and looted public offices. John of Gaunt owned substantial land in and around Ringmer. As the younger brother of the Black Prince and uncle to King Richard he had accumulated a large amount of land throughout England. John Delves, who was custodian of Gaunt's estates in Ringmer, was roughly treated and the records of his lord's estates and all transactions were taken from him and ceremoniously burned on the village green.

During the Civil War (1642–51), the village of Ringmer once more played an important part in history. The villagers supported the Parliamentarians or Roundheads. William Penn's father-in-law was a Roundhead officer who lost his life at the siege of Arundel. The Roundhead soldiers were known for their somber attire and strong religious beliefs. On the other side, King Charles I and his cavalier soldiers reveled in the finer things of life such as velvet clothes, thigh high boots and feathered hats. The atmosphere was ripe for change and most people in the country took a stand in one camp or the other.

A major occupation during the Civil War was the poaching of the king's deer. The Roundheads unmercifully hunted the deer around the village of Ringmer until they were almost extinct.

The social climate changed again early in the 19th century as men returned from the Napoleonic Wars and found their country in the grips of economic collapse. There were many people on the verge of starvation because of bad harvests and uncooperative weather. Workhouses for the poor came into effect that mostly housed women and children. The conditions were appalling and many people did not survive, especially the children who worked as long as 10 hours a day.

In Ringmer, about 20 men had been incarcerated or transported for the act of poaching that they felt was not only their right but also their privilege. As they returned from the penal colonies, they set about changing the economic climate in England and the beginnings of a trade union began. George Loveless, a man from another county, was a prominent leader for the movement that began in the south of England and spread quickly to the rest of the country. In 1830, hundreds of men were arrested and sent to trial in East Sussex. While some were transported to the colonies, others were incarcerated and nine were sentenced to death, but this did not stop the union forming. They continued to fight the government by demanding a fair day's pay for a full day of work. It is not known for sure if union members sent threatening letters to the farmers to use laborers instead of threshing machines, but the intimidation worked.

The first mention of the Captain Swing letters was in the Times newspaper on October 21, 1830. The anonymous letters were sent to farmers advising them not to use their equipment and deprive a man of a day's work. Reprisals would be in the form of arson, as the equipment would be burnt to the ground. The letters were sometimes written with an illiterate hand and others were scholarly in nature but they were all signed Captain Swing in remembrance of those men who had died for their beliefs swinging from the gallows.

## What to see and do today:

The village was originally called Ringmere, which is an Old English word-meaning ring of pools. There is no evidence that there were several pools around the village but it was mentioned in the Domesday Book of 1086 as a thriving community.

The village has strong ties to the United States because of the William Penn and John Harvard connections. John Harvard graduated from Cambridge College receiving a B. A. in 1631 and a M. A. in 1636. He had a good friend at college called John Sadler who was the son of a Vicar at Ringmer village. There were many occasions when Harvard went to stay with Sadler during half terms and other school holidays. It was most likely during one of these visits that he met and fell in love with Sadler's sister, Ann. They were married on April 19, 1636 and sailed to the New World early the following year. Their lives together would be short lived because John died two years later after a short illness on September 14, 1638. Ann remarried just over a year later to the Rev. Thomas Allen and it was the reverend who took control of the financial affairs of John Harvard's estate.

Penn came from an influential Church of England family who sent him to Christ's Church, Oxford College in 1660. He was expelled in 1662 because of religious nonconformity. At 25 years of age, he became a Quaker and was arrested several times for his heretic teachings. In 1672, he met and married Gulielma Springett, a local girl from Ringmer. In 1677, Penn left for the Colonies and a new life free from persecution. Penn's father negotiated a settlement in New Jersey in return for a large loan owed to him by King Charles II. It is believed the king was grateful that the Quakers would be settled in the Colonies and as far away from his kingdom as possible.

The area allocated for the Quakers was south and west of New Jersey. Penn gave it the name of "Sylvania" but King Charles changed it and called it Pennsylvania. Unfortunately, while he was in America, Penn's financial advisor, Philip Ford, so badly misused his patron's funds that Penn was almost bankrupt. He was on the brink of financial ruin and almost lost Pennsylvania. He returned to England in 1701 to defend himself and spent the next 10 years in various court battles, fighting to regain his rightful possessions. He suffered a stroke in 1712, leaving his care and responsibilities to his family.

In the 1920s the American ambassador unveiled the village sign of Ringmer in honor and recognition of the village's association with the history and development of America.

It was on greens such as Ringmer during medieval times that the term "Pay Cash on the Nail" came into being. Wooden posts were set up with a shallow metal bowl nailed to the post. These were known as "nails." The money owed would be placed in the bowl in full view of everyone around who witnessed the transaction, and insured that the debt or taxes had been paid in full.

## Food for thought:
### The Cock Inn
The Cock Inn is a wonderful 16th-century inn on the Uckfield Road just a couple of miles from Ringmer. The inn is mentioned in several Good Pub guides and is regarded by the local folk as the best place to eat and drink in the area. The inn provides traditional pub food as well as specialty dishes. They also offer a fine selection of wines, ales and beers.
Telephone: (0) 1273 812040. Address: Uckfield Road, Ringmer.

## If you decide to stay:
### Broyle Place
Broyle Place has a long history and is a magnificent manor house. It has a partial moat that is surrounded by beautiful lawns and well-tended gardens. Many notable families of history have owned the property, such as the Archbishop of Canterbury and Sir William Springett, whose youngest daughter married William Penn. The manor house was also the hunting lodge of Queen Elizabeth I. There are two rooms available at Broyle Place: the King's Suite and the Queen's Room. Both rooms have bathrooms en suite with tea and coffee facilities, hairdryers and a delicious, full English breakfast.
 Telephone: (0) 1273 814334. Address: Broyle Place, Ringmer.

## How to get there:
There is indirect train service from London Victoria and Charing Cross to Ringmer via Lewes. Travel time is approximately 1 hour and 30 minutes.
**By car**: Take A21 south out of London to Tonbridge. In Tonbridge take A26 towards Lewes. Just north of Lewes

take B2192 on the left to Ringmer. Ringmer is approximately 58 miles away from central London.

## Neighboring places of interest:
### Glyndebourne House
The first Glyndebourne Festival was launched on May 28th, 1934, and was organized by John Christie, who inherited the estate at Glyndebourne in 1920. He and his wife Audrey Mildmay, a professional singer, felt that opera was almost nonexistent in England outside of London and decided to do something about it.

They built on their grounds at Glyndebourne a 300-seat theatre with an orchestra pit and a stage that included modern technical and lighting equipment. Glyndebourne is also the home of the first opera house built in England since John Christie built its first theater in 1934. The new building opened in 1994, exactly 60 years after the first with a performance of the same opera, *Le nozze di Figaro*.

The young Luciano Pavarotti sang at Glyndebourne in 1964, years before The Three Tenors concerts!
Telephone: (0) 1273 815000 Information. (0) 1273 813813 Box Office.

# *Index*

Alfriston 208–216
*Anglo-Saxon Chronicles* 49, 193, 226, 229
Aylesford 157–158
Battle 2, 192–198
*Becket, St. Thomas à* 141
Biddenden 144–150
*Boadicea, Queen* 41–44
Bodiam 184–191
Bradwell-on-Sea 18
Brightling 164–166
*Britnorth, Leader of Essex* 13–14
*Brown, Lancelot "Capability"* 135–136
*Burghley, Lord* 78–80
Burwash 159–166
*Caesar, Julius* 2
Canterbury 140–143
Castle Hedingham 56–63
**CASTLES:**
    Castle Bodiam, Bodiam 184–186, 188
    Chiddingstone 123
    Chilham Castle 138–139
    Colchester 45
    Hedingham 57–58
    Hever Castle Chiddingstone 128–129
    Leeds Castle 151–157
    Lewes Castle, Lewes 203–204
    Pevensey Castle 232–233
    Rochester 115–116
    Rye Castle, Rye 172
*Charles I, King* 86, 88, 89, 130, 238
Chiddingstone 119–127
Chilham 135–143
Chipping Ongar 51–52
*Churchill, Sir Winston* 100–101
**CHURCHES:**
    All Saints', Biddenden 146
    All Saints', Maldon 14–15
    All Saints', Purleigh 8
    Canterbury Cathedral, Canterbury 140–142
    Church of King Charles the Martyr, Tunbridge Wells 89
    Lullington Church, Lullington 215–216
    Rochester Cathedral, Rochester 115
    St. Andrews, Alfriston 212
    St. Andrews, Greensted-juxta-Ongar 50–51
    St. Bartholomew, Burwash 162, 166
    St. Botolph's, Hadstock 69–70

St. John the Baptist, Finchingfield  61
St. John the Baptist, St. Mary & St. Lawrence, Thaxted  73
St. Mary and St Peter's Church, Wilmington  221
St. Mary's, Chiddingstone  123–124
St. Mary's, Chilham  138–139
St. Mary's, Cobham  82–84
St. Mary's, Rye  171
St. Mary the Virgin, Dedham  22
St. Mary the Virgin, Saffron Walden  67
St. Nicholas, Castle Hedingham  59
St. Nicholas, Pluckley  132
St. Osyth's Priory, St. Osyth  28
St. Peter ad Vincula, Coggeshall  38
St. Peter and St. Paul's, St. Osyth  29
St. Peter-on-the-Wall, Bradwell-on-Sea  18
St. Thomas', Winchelsea  180
Waltham Abbey Church, Chipping Ongar  52
Clacton-on-Sea  31–32
*Claudius, Emperor*  41
Cobham  78–85
Coggeshall  33–40
Colchester  41–48
Colne Valley Railway  59
*Constable, John*  2, 20–21
*Cromwell, Oliver*  61, 67, 102
Dedham  2, 20–25
*Defoe, Daniel*  12–13
*Dickens, Charles*  109–114, 169
*Domesday Book, The*  2, 17, 20, 98, 119, 195, 197, 231
East Sussex (County)  159–243
*Edmund, King*  49–50
*Edward the Confessor, King*  177, 192, 226–227
*Edward the Elder, King*  13
*Elizabeth I, Queen*  30, 52, 58, 79, 107, 129, 130, 170, 179
English Civil War  6, 30, 45, 238
Essex (County)  5–77
*Fawkes, Guy*  78
Finchingfield  60–63
Frinton-on-Sea  32
*Frithewald, King*  26
*Fryth, John*  93–95
**GARDENS:**
Bridge End Gardens, Saffron Walden  67
Enchanted Forest & Gardens, The, Groombridge  91
Great Dixter, Northiam  191
Leeds Castle Gardens  156
Painshill Park, Cobham  83
Southover Grange & Gardens, Lewes  204
*George I, King*  167–168
Glyndebourne  243
Great Dixter  191

245

Greensted-juxta-Ongar  49–55
Groombridge  91–92
Gunpowder Plot, The  78, 80
Hadstock  69–70
*Harold, King*  2, 52
*Henry II, King*  141
*Henry VII, King*  52, 58, 59, 130, 199
*Henry VIII, King*  52, 58, 107, 126, 141, 151–155, 199–202
**HISTORIC HOMES:**
    Anne of Cleves House, Lewes  204–205
    Audley End, Saffron Walden  65–66
    Bateman House, Burwash  163
    Bull House, Lewes  205
    Chartwell House, Westerham  100
    Clergy House, Alfriston  213
    Cobham Hall, Cobham  81–82
    Great Dixter, Northiam  191
    Ightham Mote, Ivy Hatch  102–105
    Knole, Sevenoaks  107–108
    Lamb House, Rye  171
    Owletts Farmhouse, Cobham  84–85
    Paycocke's Home, Coggeshall  38
        St. Clere's Hall, St. Osyth  29
    Sherman Home, Dedham  22
    Spains Hall, Finchingfield  61–62
    Squerryes Court, Westerham  98
    Tudor Mint House, The, Pevensey  233
*Holst, Gustav*  71–72, 73
**HOTELS:**
    Berkeley House Hotel, Lewes  207
    Collina House Hotel, Tenterden  149
    Crossways Hotel, Wilmington  223
    Dean's Place Hotel, Alfriston  214
    Elvey Farm Country Hotel, Pluckley  133
    George Hotel, The, Battle  198
    George Hotel, The, Colchester  47–48
    Gordon House Hotel, Rochester  118
    Kings Arms Hotel, Westerham  99
    Oakland Hotel, Purleigh  10
    Packford Hotel, Epping Forest  54
    Rose & Crown Hotel, Colchester  48
    Royal Oak Hotel, Sevenoaks  107
    Royal Victoria & Bull Hotel, Rochester  117
    Swan Hotel, Maldon  17
    Swan Hotel, Royal Tunbridge Wells  90
    Swan Hotel, Thaxted  76
    White Hart Hotel, Lewes  206
    Woodlands Manor Hotel, Coggeshall  40
Ightham Mote  102–108
**INNS:**
    Bell Inn, The, Purleigh  9–10

    Blue Boar, Maldon  17
    Broyle Place, Ringmer  242
    Crossways Guest House, Thaxted  75
    Elms Farm, Bodiam  190
    Glydwish Place, Burwash  164
    Larkins Farm, Chiddingstone  125
    Maison Talbooth Guest House, Dedham  24
    Marlborough Head, The, Dedham  23
    Mermaid Inn, Rye  173–174
    North Hall Farm Guest House, Saffron Walden  69
    Queen's Head Inn, The, Saffron Walden  68
    Red Lion Inn, Finchingfield  62
    Rosemary Farm, Castle Hedingham  60
    Rosewood B&B, Sevenoaks  106
    Smugglers Inn, The, Alfriston  214
    Smugglers Inn, The, Pevensey  235
    Star Inn, The, Alfriston  215
    Stour Valley House, Chilham  140
    Strand House, The, Winchelsea  183
    Sun Inn, Saffron Walden  67
    Tudor Cottage, Biddenden  147
    Vicarage, The, Rye  174
    Wilmington Priory, Wilmington  222
    Ye Olde Leather Bottle Hotel, Cobham  83
*James, Henry*  168–170
*James I, King*  80-81, 91, 130
*John, King*  56–57
Kent (County)  78–158
Kent and East Sussex Railway, Bodiam  189
*Kipling, Rudyard*  159–163, 170
Leeds Castle  151–158
Lewes  199–207
Little Dunmow  76–77
Lullington  215–216
*Magna Carta, The*  57
Maldon  7, 12–19
Manningtree  24–25
Michelham Priory, Wilmington  224–225
**MILLS:**
    Bourne Mill, Colchester  46
    Finchingfield Windmill, Finchingfield  60–61
    Thaxted Windmill, Thaxted  75
**MUSEUMS:**
    Canterbury Heritage Museum, Canterbury  142
    Canterbury Roman Museum, Canterbury  142
    Charles Dickens Museum, Rochester  114
    Colchester Castle  45
    Colne Valley Railway, Castle Hedingham  59
    Court House Museum, Winchelsea  180
    Maldon District Museum, Maldon  16
    Museum of Local History, Battle  197

    North Weald Aerodrome Museum, North Weald  54
    Royal Tunbridge Wells Museum & Art Gallery  89–90
    Rye Castle Museum, Rye  172
    Saffron Walden Museum, Saffron Walden  68
**NATURE:**
    Bridge End Gardens, Saffron Walden  67
    Colchester Zoo  45
    Leeds Castle Aviary  156
    Royal Epping Forest  52–53
    Turf Maze, Saffron Walden  68
*Paine, Thomas*  205
*Paycocke, John*  34
*Penn, William*  236, 240–241
Pevensey  2, 226–235
Pluckley  128–134
**PUBS:**
    Black Horse, The, Pluckley  132
    Jolly Sailor, The, Maldon  17
    Plough, The, Ivy Hatch  106
    Queen's Head, The, Maldon  17
    Queen's Head, The, Purleigh  10
    Red Lion, St. Osyth  31
    Rose and Crown, Burwash  163–164
    Royal Oak, The, Chipping Ongar  54
    White Horse, The, Chilham  139
    Wool Pack Pub, Coggeshall  39
    Ye Olde Leather Bottle Hotel, Cobham  83
Purleigh  5–11
**RAILFAN INTEREST:**
    Colne Valley Railway  59
    Kent and East Sussex Railway, Bodiam  189
    Spa Valley Railway  90
    Tenterden Town Station  149
**RESTAURANTS:**
    Brokers Arms, Royal Tunbridge Wells  90
    Castle Inn, Bodiam  190
    Castle Inn, Chiddingstone  124
    Cock Inn, The, Ringmer  242
    Crown Inn, The, Groombridge  92
    Dering Arms, Pluckley  133
    Fairfax Hall, Leeds Castle  157
    Giant's Rest, The, Wilmington  222
    Grasshopper Inn, Westerham  99
    Jack Fuller's Restaurant, The, Brightling  165–166
    Old Moot House, Castle Hedingham  60
    Old Needlemakers Café, Lewes  206
    Pilgrim's Rest, The, Battle  198
    Priory Restaurant, St. Osyth  31
    Smugglers Inn, The, Pevensey  234
    Ye Maydes Restaurant, Biddenden  147
    Ye Olde Curiousitie Restaurant, Rochester  117

Richard II, King  237
Ringmer  236–243
Rochester  109–118
Royal Epping Forest  52–53
Royal Tunbridge Wells  86–92
Rye  167–174
Saffron Walden  64–70
*St. Osyth*  1, 26–27
St. Osyth  26–32
Sevenoaks  107–108
Spa Valley Railway  90
**TEA ROOMS:**
    Cake Table Tea Room, Thaxted  75
    Causeway Tea Rooms, The, Finchingfield  62
    Claris's Tea Room, Biddenden  147
    Clock House Tea Rooms, Coggeshall  40
    Essex Rose Tea Room, Dedham  23
    Old Weavers' Tea Room, Canterbury  143
    Peggotty's Tea Shop, Tenterden  149
    Swan Cottage Tea Rooms, Rye  173
    Tea Tree, The, Winchelsea  182
    Tilly's Tea Rooms, Colchester  47
    Ye Olde Curiousitie Tea Shop, Rochester  117
Tenterden  148–149
Thaxted  71–77
Tunbridge Wells, see Royal Tunbridge Wells
*Turpin, Dick*  52
*Tyndale, William*  93–96
Vikings, The  13–14, 27, 49, 192, 229
**VINEYARDS:**
    Biddenden Vineyards & Cider Works, 146
    New Hall, Purleigh  9
    Tenterden Vineyard, Tenderden  150
**WALKS:**
    Alfriston  213
    Dedham  22–23
    Frinton-on-Sea  32
    1066 Country Walks, Battle  197
    1066 Walks, Pevensey  234
    Winchelsea  181
*Washington, George*  5
*Washington, Lawrence*  1, 5–7, 8, 14–15
*Wells, H.G.*  169–170
Westerham  93–101
*William the Conqueror, King*  2, 20, 56, 119, 151, 162, 192–195, 196, 226–232
Wilmington  217–224
Winchelsea  175–183
*Wolfe, James, General*  98

## About the Author

Elizabeth Wallace writes and speaks extensively about travel and history, and she has combined these two interests in *Extraordinary Places Close to London*. She has created a unique travel book that provides intriguing insight into the history of 30 towns and villages with essential travel information.

Elizabeth was born in England and is a member of the Society of Women Writers and Journalists, one of the oldest societies for professional writers in Britain. She immigrated to the United States in 1978 and now lives in Colorado where she is very active in the local literary community. In addition to her three books, Elizabeth has written for an award-winning Colorado historical magazine, and makes regular radio and television appearances to discuss topics such as the origin of everyday words, history, and travel.

Elizabeth founded the Castle Rock Writers and is a member of Colorado Center for the Book.

www.extraordinaryplaces.net